INTRODUCTION TO
AUTOMATED DATA PROCESSING

INTRODUCTION TO
AUTOMATED
DATA PROCESSING

ROBERT G. LANGENBACH

Professor
School of Business Administration
San Diego State College

PRENTICE-HALL, INC., Englewood Cliffs, N.J.

PRENTICE-HALL INTERNATIONAL, INC., London
PRENTICE-HALL OF AUSTRALIA, PTY. LTD., Sydney
PRENTICE-HALL OF CANADA, LTD., Toronto
PRENTICE-HALL OF INDIA PRIVATE LTD., New Delhi
PRENTICE-HALL OF JAPAN, INC., Tokyo

Library of Congress Catalog Card Number 68-11404
Printed in the United States of America

Current printing (last digit):

10   9   8   7   6   5   4   3   2   1

PREFACE

If you have little or no knowledge of automated data processing operations but have the desire to become acquainted with some of the data processing devices and procedures that are a part of your daily life, then this book is meant for you. After you have completed this book, you will not qualify as an expert computer programmer, a system analyst, or even a key punch operator—but you will have eliminated many of the mysteries of modern data processing and will have discovered whether or not you are sufficiently interested to continue study and perhaps pursue a career in automated data processing. This book does not present an exhaustive study of specific topics—it serves only as an exposure to some of the basic principles and applications of automated data processing and does not emphasize machine technology. No handling of any equipment is necessary. Generalizations pertaining to basic operating procedures for various automated data processing media are followed by simplified applications of those media. Only when it is desirable to understand the "how" of an operation is any description presented of machine technology. After the introduction to basic understandings applicable to all data processing in the first chapter, the following chapters acquaint you with various systems in which the processing principles are applied. It is suggested that you review the introductory chapter after you have finished Chapters 2, 3, and 4.

Robert G. Langenbach

CONTENTS

1 INTRODUCTION 1

INTRODUCTION   1
BASIC TERMINOLOGY IN AUTOMATED
   DATA PROCESSING   2
DATA PROCESSING CYCLE   8
AUTOMATED DATA PROCESSING
   FUNCTIONS   13
GOALS OF AUTOMATED DATA
   PROCESSING   17
REVIEW QUESTIONS   22

**IS&M2 INTERRELATIONSHIPS OF SYSTEMS AND
MACHINES   25**

INTRODUCTION   25
PEGBOARDS   27
KEYSORTING   29
METAL PLATES   34
MICROFILMING   38
REVIEW QUESTIONS   44

vii

IDP 3   INTEGRATED DATA PROCESSING   47

INTRODUCTION   47
PUNCHED CARDS   48
PUNCHED CARD PORT-A-PUNCH   80
MARKED-SENSED CARDS   82
APERTURE CARDS   85
PUNCHED TAGS AND TICKETS   88
BINARY DECIMAL NUMBERING
    SYSTEM   92
PUNCHED TAPE   97
EDGE-PUNCHED CARDS   108
MAGNETIC TAPES   114
REVIEW QUESTIONS   116

EDP 4   ELECTRONIC DATA PROCESSING   123

INTRODUCTION   123
PROGRAMMING CONCEPT   124
DIAGRAMMING CONCEPT   141
CODING CONCEPT   146
INPUT   150
STORAGE   156
CONTROL UNIT   170
ARITHMETIC UNIT   172
OUTPUT UNIT   174
SUMMARY   176
EXPLANATION OF MODEL PROGRAM
    FOR PAYROLL ON IMCOM   182
MICR-MAGNETIC INK CHARACTER
    RECOGNITION   194
OPTICAL READERS   201
REVIEW QUESTIONS   209

5 **AUTOMATED DATA PROCESSING PERSONNEL PROBLEMS** **221**

INTRODUCTION   221
EMPLOYMENT PROBLEMS   223
MORALE PROBLEMS   226
TRAINING PROBLEMS   227
CONCLUSION   229
REVIEW QUESTIONS   230

INDEX   **233**

INTRODUCTION TO
AUTOMATED DATA PROCESSING

1

INTRODUCTION

When the history of our age is written, it will record three profoundly important technological developments: (1) nuclear energy, which tremendously increases the amount of energy available to do the world's work; (2) automation, which greatly increases man's ability to use tools; and (3) the computer, which multiplies man's ability to do mental work.*

Before you finish reading this book, two important factors will be apparent:

1. Data processing involves much more than the use of multi-million dollar high-speed electronic computers.
2. There is no reason to fear and evade studying data processing because the subject is difficult.

Twenty years ago, electronic data processing was relatively unknown and was rarely discussed among businessmen. Since World War II, business has developed an exciting new concept in processing data. Yet although we are in constant contact with this new concept (by way of credit cards, utility bills, sales tickets, etc.), very few people are sufficiently acquainted with modern data processing methods to be able to discuss the subject intelligently.

Along with this new concept of data processing has come a new language heretofore unknown to even executive managers in business organizations. The language and its concepts are so revolution-

---

* Ralph Cordiner, President, General Electric Company, quoted by K. G. Matheson, "The Impact of the Computer on Curricula of Colleges of Business Administration," *Collegiate News and Views*, XIV, No. 4 (May, 1961), p. 3.

ary their descriptive terms are not standardized. Because terms mean different things to different people, we encounter still another block in discussing data processing. Nevertheless, a totally new era in data processing is upon us; and unless we learn to understand these new concepts, we shall find that the advancing business world has left us in its dust. For example, it is almost impossible to glance at a current business or news periodical without finding several advertisements and articles discussing newly developed data processing procedures and equipment. One of the leading and most profitable businesses in the United States today is the development and production of electronic computers and other data processing equipment used in modern business offices.

BASIC TERMINOLOGY IN AUTOMATED DATA PROCESSING

In order to become acquainted with this new concept of data processing, we must understand some of the terminology frequently used in describing specific operations. As the terms are not yet standardized, many of them carry multiple meanings. In this book, the basic data processing words are defined as follows:

Data

Data is generally considered to be the facts and figures extracted from direct observation by the persons using the data. These signs and characters are said to be syntactical—they are isolated numbers, letters, words, and symbols that will later be structured into charts, tables, and reports.

Information

When data is properly combined, a meaningful conclusion called *information* is formed. The isolated numbers, words, or symbols representing data are processed to produce understandable relationships of numbers, words, and symbols on a *semantical* or meaningful level. Data, therefore, is primarily associated with input or the beginning phases of the processing; information is associated with output or the final results of the processing.

Data Processing

Actually, data has been processed since prehistoric times; barter of personal and consumer goods, counting beads, calculating with the Chinese abacus are but three examples. But within the past score of years a comparatively new concept of data processing has arisen. Today, the term *data processing* in business implies (1) acceptance, (2) rearrangement, (3) refinement of data (isolated numbers and words) into a form of information (charts, tables, and reports) to be used by businessmen who are responsible for making business decisions and formulating company policies. Converting data into information often involves many separate processes, such as originating, itemizing, manipulating, presenting, and disposing (see pp. 9–12 for a more detailed description of these processes).

System

"System" is probably the most loosely used word in the new data processing language—a kind of "all-things-to-all-people" word. Basically, a data processing system implies a preplanned combination of operations and procedures, personnel, and equipment by which a prescribed goal or objective may be accomplished. Most definitions of a system assume a degree of interrelationship of the components that make up the organized whole or the goal which is to be achieved.

Perhaps the key word throughout the entire data processing language is "interrelationship." For any specific operation to be efficient, it must fit in with the operations that occurred before it and with those that will occur after. For example, a system (a preplanned method to complete a specific job) would probably not be efficient if data was first typed by a secretary in the order department, another form typed in the shipping department, and still another form typed in the accounting (billing) department. Perhaps it would have been preferable to have had the data typed only once, by the secretary in the order department, but to have had carbon copies made for the other two departments. If such a procedure was to be followed, the interrelationships of all three departments would have to be closely reviewed so that each department would receive all the necessary data it required from the single typing operation—typing the form in the order department.

The one typed form would have to contain all the data needed by each department.

Typing the form in each separate department, as just described, was a "system" because it was preplanned in terms of operations and procedures, personnel, and equipment, but it was a *poor* system because it did not carefully consider the interrelationships of the other two departments. The second, carbon-paper system—and it, too, was a system—did consider the interrelationships of the departments and thereby permitted a reduction of effort and expense and provided an increase in the accuracy of the typed data through eliminating unnecessary typing.

IS&M—Interrelationships of Systems and Machines

In order to look at some data processing operations commonly used in business but not employing certain types of electronic devices, we shall call this elementary group of operations *IS&M*—Interrelationships of Systems and Machines. This term is not as universally accepted as IDP (Integrated Data Processing) or EDP (Electronic Data Processing), terms to be analyzed later; but we should become acquainted with some basic and simplified concepts and operations which cannot be included in IDP or EDP.

IS&M (Interrelationships of Systems and Machines) involve consideration of two factors: (1) the system being followed (the planned method to arrive at a goal), (2) the equipment (machines or devices) being used. IS&M implies that the relationship between the system and the machines should reduce or eliminate unnecessary steps, speed up one or more steps in the process, and increase the accuracy of the information.

Changing office equipment to fit in with an established system may be no better an answer to the problem of improving operations than would be changing a system to fit in with existing equipment. Goals, personnel, and procedures must be reviewed and analyzed, along with an analysis of equipment needed to complete the operations.

Machines or devices generally included in IS&M are pegboards, typewriters, photocopiers, calculators, duplicators, intercoms, television, and other equipment that does not require punched cards, punched tapes, or magnetic tapes.

IDP—Integrated Data Processing

Integrated data processing (IDP) is a relatively new concept in processing business data. Actually, IDP is an extension of IS&M. Various machines are used to eliminate handling data by recording the data only once, generally at its source or origin, and to employ the recorded data in a variety of ways, in a variety of machines, and in more than one department within a business. Recall the previous example, using carbon paper in IS&M to eliminate additional typing of sales data. Both IS&M and IDP attempt to capture all the necessary data at the point of origin; IDP is also concerned with placing the captured data in various media and with using a machine language that is common or understandable to all machines that will process these various media. Some of the common-language media most often used are

Punched cards

Punched-edge cards

Punched tags and tickets

Punched tapes

Magnetic inks

IDP further differs from IS&M in being concerned with the mechanical processing of data, whereas IS&M pertains more to human operations after the original data is recorded. In IS&M, a human being will read and interpret the data typed on the sales order previously discussed. An IDP operation attempts to eliminate human searching, interpreting, and recording of data by supplying the data in a common-language media that can then be fed to various machines as a device that permits the machines to "talk" or communicate with one another. The theory behind an IDP operation is coordination of various data processing machines in a continuous and automatic operation that accepts and processes data from its point of origin to the desired goal. Basically, then, IDP is characterized by three distinct features:

1. The original data is recorded at its point of origin in a complete form so that no additional referrals to the source documents will be necessary.

2. The data is recorded in a common language acceptable to various machines that will process the data.

3. The data is processed by mechanical rather than human operations.

We can now define IDP as a comprehensive procedure of recording data at its point of origin in a common machine language compatible to all machines that will process the data. By definition, the goal of IDP is to mold all related data to be processed into a harmonious and efficient whole.

EDP—Electronic Data Processing

The term *electronic data processing* (EDP) is somewhat misleading, for the equipment used in IDP and some machines in IS&M are also electronic. What, then, is the distinguishing characteristic of EDP? The electronic computer! When a computer is added to the processing of data, the classification of IDP is changed to EDP. We must remember, however, that EDP is not an electronic computer alone but includes all the necessary equipment used in IDP processing plus the computer.

An EDP system is generally characterized by a high rate of speed and by self-containment of various processes to be completed. EDP can complete any combination or sequence of operations that any other group of office machines can complete, but because a computer is included, data is processed at much greater speeds and with less human intervention between the various stages of processing.

Mechanization

Data processing procedures are mechanized when machines which can perform only one or two functions are combined to produce a data processing system; the human operator continues to serve as the communication link between the various machines needed in the system. IS&M is usually mechanized (for example, an electric typewriter) but seldom automated. IDP becomes less mechanized and more automated (for example, an electric typewriter that produces a punched tape which can be used in other machines to provide data). EDP is usually automated but seldom mechanized (for example, an optical scanner that provides data directly to the computer without human intervention). Thus, as the transition is made from IS&M to IDP to EDP, mechanization and human handling of data decrease and automation increases.

Automation

Automation, as used in data processing, implies a degree of machine control that is self-starting, self-checking, and self-stopping. Whenever a deviation from a prescribed and preplanned pattern occurs, the machine corrects the deviation or prevents the processing from continuing, and the checking or stopping is done by the machine with no need of human supervision. A household thermostat is an example of an automatic device; without human attention, it will start and stop the flow of heat so as to maintain a predetermined temperature. A computer is likewise self-directing, and thus it is classified as "automatic."

> The term *automation* designates one of the most important characteristics of an automatic computer: the ability to guide and control itself during the course of its data processing action. That is, once the human operator has set up the computer to operate, the machine takes over control of itself. . . . The machine is self-directing, but only within definite prescribed limits which must be predetermined by the human operator during the setup of the machine for operation.*

Many persons engaged in data processing prefer to use the term *automated data processing* (ADP) rather than electronic data processing (EDP). Actually, electronics is not always a necessary condition for automation, and the term *electronic* obscures the more fundamental factors of automation.

If we accept the foregoing definition of *automation*, we can see that the term *office automation* so commonly found in business writings is a misnomer. We have not yet reached a stage in data

---

* Ned Chapin, *An Introduction to Automatic Computers* (Princeton, N.J.: D. Van Nostrand Company, Inc., 1957), p. 7.

processing where, as the term *office automation* would imply, we have a completely unmanned office in which *all* the work is done by machines and no human supervision or effort is necessary. Automation in the office, yes; office automation, no!

Summary of Terminology

From the preceding discussion, the progression of data processing classification would appear as follows:

AUTOMATED DATA PROCESSING

(IS&M) Interrelationships of Systems and Machines	(IDP) Integrated Data Processing	(EDP) Electronic Data Processing
Human-operated machines or devices performing a separate and complete operation as part of a system.	Machines producing a common-language media applicable to other machines in the system.	Machines using a common-language media—one machine of which is an electronic computer.

Note that the term *automation* is not specifically assigned to any one of the classifications, but each of the data processing classifications does contain some element of automation. IS&M, for example, may include an electric typewriter which automatically continues to print underscores so long as the typist keeps the underscore key depressed; it is not necessary to depress the key for each individual underscore mark. Also, the return of the typebars into the cradle position after the keys have been depressed and the letters printed on the paper is automatic because the human operator need not release the key to return the typebar to its correct position; it returns automatically. The new IBM Selectric typewriter applies automation one step further by keeping in temporary storage the sequence in which the keys were depressed and releasing one letter at a time; no tie-up of keys is possible since the machine permits the release of one and only one letter at a time.

DATA PROCESSING CYCLE

Handling data in office procedures is commonly explained in a series of five steps and is often referred to as the *data processing cycle.* Most of us are aware of the procedures required to perform simple business transactions, such as the writing of a personal check, but rarely do we categorize the steps involved. We need not be fully aware of what the various steps in our daily routines require; but being able to classify the specific functions will help us to understand, analyze, and evaluate methods and procedures used to process data. The following five steps comprise the data processing cycle:

1. Originating data *in* source documents

2. Recording or itemizing data *from* source documents

3. Processing (manipulating) itemized data

4. Producing a final record or answer (summarizing)

5. Storing (filing) the summary or record for future reference.

Origination of Data

As noted earlier (p. 2), the beginning phases of data processing deal with *data* (isolated facts and figures that will later be classified, sorted, computed, and summarized to represent meaningful information). These basic figures or data are placed on various forms and records that will be used to provide the "raw" or initial data at the beginning of the data processing cycle. The form or record containing the data at the start of the cycle is called a *source document.* What is produced as the final form or answer depends on what data was taken from the document, then classified, sorted, computed, and reported. For example, assume that a group of people wish to elect officers for their organization, and the election to an office requires a majority vote. To conduct the election, de-

| BALLOT |
| (Mark one) |
| |
| PRESIDENT |
| Mr. Jones ⊠ |
| Mr. Black ☐ |
| Mr. Smith ☐ |

signated persons will distribute the proper ballots to members of the organization. After the members have indicated their preference by checking one of the candidates' names listed on the ballot, the inserted "X" (data) on the ballot will then classify the ballot as a source document. From these ballots, or source documents, the data will be extracted, processed, and reported. The first step, the origination of data on source documents, will have been completed.

Itemization of Data

For convenience, data from source documents is often transferred to summary forms to permit easier interpretation and manipulation. Often, the second step of the data processing cycle merely involves tabulating or listing the various data appearing on

```
TALLY SHEET
Mr. Jones ||||| ||||| ||||| |

Mr. Black ||||| |||||

Mr. Smith ||||
```

collected source documents. Would it not be easier to handle the election procedures if the marked ballots were tallied one at a time on a summary sheet rather than having someone try to retain a running count in his mind? Listing or tabulating ballots in a manner that facilitates the final evaluation of the totals illustrates the second step of the data processing cycle.

Manipulation of Data

The third step of the cycle is the manipulative or computational step. After the original data has been extracted from the source documents and conveniently listed or summarized, the arithmetic functions (addition, subtraction, multiplication, and division) are applied. This step, the computational step, receives the greatest attention within the data processing cycle. Ten-key adding machines, rotary calculators, key-driven calculators, bookkeeping ma-

```
Mr. Jones =  16
Mr. Black =  10
Mr. Smith =   4
  Total Vote  30

For a majority:

      Total Vote ÷ 2
          30 ÷ 2 = 15

Elected: Mr. Jones
      (more than ½)
```

chines, accounting machines—these are but a few of the devices which may be used to assist clerks in the manipulative phase of the cycle. In our ballot example in which election requires a majority vote, the third step of the cycle would require that the total number of ballots cast be counted and then be divided by two so that the median could be ascertained and compared to the total votes received by each candidate. No candidate would be the winner until he had received more than 50 percent of the votes.

Presentation of Information

Reporting is the fourth step in the data processing cycle. The reporting phase (see p. 3) is primarily concerned with *information* (the representation of facts and figures in meaningful summaries or conclusions). This step, the answer or solution, is the reason for

```
MINUTES OF MEETING

The meeting was called to order
at 2:00 p.m. on May 3.

Mr. Jones was elected President
of the organization.
```

processing the original data taken from the source documents. After the elections have been concluded so that one candidate has received more than 50 percent of the votes (a majority) and all offices have been filled, some report must be written by a designated person, such as the secretary to the organization. The results of the balloting would be summarized in the report or minutes of the meeting.

Disposition of Information

The final step in the data processing cycle concerns the disposition of the reports or summaries completed through the previous four steps. Depending upon the type of information and its importance, the record or written summaries may or may not be filed for

future reference. Nevertheless, whether the derived information is to be retained or disposed of constitutes a problem to be solved; hence it is assigned a step in the data processing cycle. Perhaps the minutes containing the results of the election are to be retained. But the data processing cycle is not complete until it is decided either to file the election report or minutes or to throw them away.

	Payroll check	Merchandise inventory	Merchandise sale on credit
Step 1 Source document	TIME CARD Mon ___ ___ Tue ___ ___ Wed ___ ___ Thu ___ ___ Fri ___ ___ Sat ___ ___ Total Hrs ___	REQUISITION Item No. Quantity ___ ___ ___ ___ ___ ___ Dept.	SALES TICKET TO: ___ ___ Items Purchased: ___ ___ ___ ___
Step 2 Interpretation	PAYROLL REGISTER Name Reg OT Total ___	ITEM DISBURSEMENT Dept: ___ Date: ___ Items: Quantity: ___ ___ ___ ___ ___ ___ ___ ___	ACCOUNT REGISTER Name Amount ___ ___ ___ ___ ___ ___ ___ ___
	Net pay calculations	Stock control	Sales calculations
Step 3 Calculation	Hours worked multiplied by hourly rate minus deductions	Beginning inventory minus issued items plus purchased items equals ending inventory	Total credit sales minus return sales

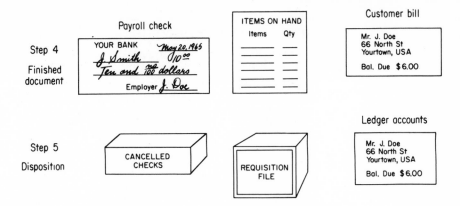

The illustrations of common data-processing operations which precede will help clarify the various steps included within each data processing cycle.

AUTOMATED DATA PROCESSING FUNCTIONS

Basically, the data processing cycle previously described is applicable to automated data processing; here, however, the processing categories have rather different names, and the processes are more mechanized than the usual manual processes used in the common data processing cycle. Instead of the five basic steps comprising the regular data processing cycle, automated data processing usually categorizes the basic procedures into the following three functions:

1. Input
2. Manipulation (processing)
3. Output.

Input

COLLECTION. Obtaining data from available source documents is the first major task in input operations. In business operations, the input volume is often quite extensive; yet it may still be only a small portion of the total volume of data that must be handled or processed before the output report can be produced. For example, bank processing of checking accounts requires considerable volume of input (each check written must be processed); but this volume is relatively small when compared to the vast amount of facts and figures already stored within a computer. A record of every previously written check for every checking account must be maintained; new checks must be included in the records; and a new or up-dated balance must be computed each day of the business week.

The input phase of automated data processing often starts with the collection of data by a manual operation, such as punching cards or paper tapes, or recording on magnetic tapes. Because human error is such a paramount factor in data processing, it is necessary to be careful that human operations be accurate. Various checks, mechanical and human, must be incorporated within the system to improve data accuracy. We must be constantly aware that automated data processing includes a "common language," such as a code in a punched card, in a punched tape, or on a magnetic tape. Once the input data represented by a specific code is transferred from the source documents to the common-language media, although the data on the cards or tapes may be used several times by different equipment, for different purposes, and at different intervals, no additional reference to the original source document should be necessary. Therefore, it is most important that all necessary data be recorded during the original coding process and that all data be accurately encoded.

VERIFICATION. The degree of accuracy required of input operations dictates the extent to which data must be verified (proofread and checked) in terms of entries, completeness of data, and acceptability of data.

Correctness. Entries need not always be 100 percent correct. Some errors in words are tolerable because other connecting letters within the words or other adjoining words will show the proper and intended meaning. For example, a punched card containing the words NEW YORK CTIY, NEW YORK in an address could easily be understood even though one word was misspelled—the common relationships reveal the desired meaning. But suppose an order for 1,610 feet of copper tubing was read from a purchase order and punched into a card as 1,160 feet instead of 1,610—the numerical relationship in this case does not reveal the correct meaning. Therefore, because numerical errors are less tolerable, greater emphasis is placed on verifying numbers than on verifying words.

Completeness. The completeness of entries implies that future reference to source documents will not be necessary if the original entry is all-inclusive. A complete entry may include (1) name (or identification number) of the person or the organization, (2) date of the transaction, (3) quantity involved, (4) identification of the element or item involved. A sales order, for example, may read

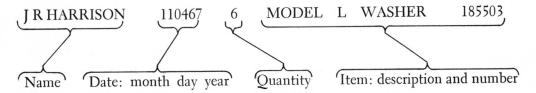

J R HARRISON   110467   6   MODEL L WASHER   185503

Name   Date: month day year   Quantity   Item: description and number

Of course, different types of transactions require that different amounts and different types of data be recorded. It is not to be assumed, however, that all data appearing on a source document must always be encoded into the common-language media, such as punched cards, punched tapes, magnetic tapes, etc. If we may reasonably assume that some of the data on the source documents will *never* be required for future data processing, then it is a waste of time and human effort to record them. Completeness of data means that we record all *required* data and omit all nonrequired data.

ACCEPTABILITY. To be acceptable, recorded data must be plausible and reasonable. If a number appears within a word (example: NEW YO8K) or a letter within a number (example: DATE 02 1K 67), the errors are quite evident. If data is not within a normal range, it is intolerable. Additional processing will only escalate the error. (Example: if employee identification numbers are always four digits or less and the largest possible number is 9999, and if a number of 19614 is recorded, an implausible mistake has been made and the processing should be halted.)

Because human error still remains a problem in input operations several new devices have been developed that can automatically collect data from source documents and transfer it to cards or tapes without any human operations. Some examples of this direct input operation are (1) magnetic ink printing on checks that can be magnetized, read, and converted into suitable data processing codes when the checks are processed (see pp. 194–201); (2) punched tags or tickets on merchandise that may be taken from the merchandise at the time of sale and then fed to a reader device that interprets the coded punches and compiles the necessary information to update the inventory (see pp. 88–92); (3) time cards that are automatically punched when inserted into a time clock so that payroll processing may be facilitated for each pay period. Currently being developed are "character-reading" devices capable of reading printed words on a page of a book or manual, translating the words automatically, and printing the translations into another language—some Russian technical journals have been translated into English without any human assistance.

Manipulation

In automated data processing the manipulation of data normally includes the rearrangement and processing of data.

REARRANGEMENT of data is usually included in the overall processing procedure. Data is usually taken from the source document and coded into a common language in the same sequence in which it appears on the document; but this sequence of input data may have to be changed to a sequence more appropriate for processing. A general rule to follow when coding data into punched cards or tape or onto magnetic tape is to record the data from the source documents in exactly the same sequence as it appears and is read from the source document. As previously noted, however, human handling of data often results in inaccuracies. To reduce errors, human operators should devote all their attention to entering the data accurately rather than need to search the source document for the needed data and make necessary interpretations; because of this accuracy element, data usually appears on punched cards and other media in the same sequence as it appears on the source documents. But since this sequence may not be the one most desirable for computation, it may be necessary to make some changes in the arrangement of the data during the processing.

PROCESSING of data includes the entire scope of operations from the input of data to the output of information. Excluding the operations needed for data origination, data arrangement, and information output, the processing of data may include the following:

1. Four arithmetic functions (addition, subtraction, multiplication, and division)

2. Comparison of numeric values as a means for making mechanical operation decisions

3. Storage of values

4. Verification of accuracy through various mechanical checks

5. Other operations necessary to perform tasks, such as computing payrolls, updating files, or storing or locating data in statistical tables.

Output

The preparation of reports or records containing the desired information comprises the output operation. The information required and the manner in which it is recorded are the two important factors to be determined before the input operations can begin. What is included on the print-out records will be determined by the purpose of the entire processing procedure. The printout could be payroll checks, lists of updated inventories, information on registration cards, or perhaps merely a list of facts and figures to be evaluated by businessmen when formulating future policy or arriving at appropriate business decisions.

In the past, output operations have been hampered by comparatively slow printing processes; but high-speed printers now can print 170,000 characters per minute, or, in terms of typewritten words, 34,000 words per minute (many of us are quite proud when we type 60 words per minute).

GOALS OF AUTOMATED DATA PROCESSING

Basically, automated data processing (ADP) attempts to satisfy two fundamental goals (1) reducing costs of information, (2) providing better information in terms of importance and speed.

As we shall see in Chapter 5, whether automated data processing has cut labor costs remains controversial. Probably we can accept the theory that ADP will result in fewer clerical workers, but workers who are retained by companies installing ADP systems will be upgraded in their position and responsibilities. And upgrading employee responsibilities usually is the basis for increasing wages.

Perhaps a larger source of savings than that associated with labor costs is the reduction of unit production costs. There are four general areas applicable to lower processing costs: (1) improving methods of reading and accepting initial data; (2) eliminating intermediate processing steps; (3) eliminating repetitive tasks; (4) reducing the handling of constant data.

Improvement of Input Reading Methods

One of the most exciting developments in ADP has been the development of new equipment capable of supplying ADP systems with tremendous volumes of raw data. This new equipment helps to keep input data clear and understandable, to provide more distinct categories of data, and to test the reasonableness of the data. There are now available optical scanners (discussed on pp. 201–09) that will optically examine a prescribed part of a sales slip, shipping order, or other printed document and automatically convert the printed data into a machine language acceptable for direct processing by a computer. Manual processing, such as selecting the desired data from the documents, typewriting or tab-punching the selected data, and proofreading the typewritten or punched data, is eliminated by optical scanning devices.

For example, a credit card holder is often identified by optical scanning. Your name or numbered code pressed onto a gasoline sales slip from your credit card will never be retyped or rewritten from your purchase of gasoline to your receipt of a gasoline statement from the company that issued your credit card. An optical scanner will "read" your name or number from the sales slip and report the "reading" to a computer which will also receive data pertaining to the amount of your purchase. A printer will automatically print the information supplied to it from the computer in terms of your new monthly gasoline statement.

Elimination of Processing Steps

Many intermediate operations are eliminated when appropriate ADP systems are introduced. Although operational savings are often made at the input stage of data processing, such as the reading, typewriting, and proofreading just mentioned, considerable savings may be made in subsequent handling of data. If, for example, a magazine subscription and mailing system has been set up on punched cards, subsequent processing of the cards on an electric sorter and an electric printer could provide from the same cards a list of data, such as the following:

1. Names of subscribers living within a certain city or state

2. Names of subscribers whose subscription expires with the mailing of the next issue

3. Names of subscribers who have received the magazine for more than ten years.

Once the necessary original data has been recorded in a machine language media compatible with other processing machines in the office, extracting any of the recorded data is quite simple. The data may be called for at any desired time; it is no longer necessary to refer back to the original sources of data, such as the letters or application blanks submitted by the magazine subscribers.

Elimination of Repetitive Tasks

It is basically possible to mechanize any simple repetitive task in handling data; if the task is repeated a sufficient number of times, it may be preferable to automate the task. Much of our office work falls into simple repetitive patterns which are time-consuming and boring. If, for example, a clerk occasionally has to extract ledger cards from a company's files, it would probably be beneficial to mechanize the operation—perhaps a power-driven rotary drum file could be used by the clerk at her work station. If however, the major portion of the processing system involves finding, posting, and filing many individual ledger cards, it may be necessary for a computer to process data in coded language. Most large banks now record all pertinent data involved in producing customers' monthly bank statements in a coded form that is stored within the banks' computers. The repetitive task of manually posting each written check and each deposit slip to a customer's account has been eliminated. Thus we can see why system analysts assigned to improve a data processing operation frequently start by asking (1) *what kind* of tasks are being repeated, (2) *how often* are they being repeated.

Reduction of Handling of Constant Data

The fourth method of reducing operational costs pertains to eliminating the handling of *constant data* (data that does not change from one processing period to the next). Data processing is facilitated when attention can be directed toward the *variable* data involved (data that could possibly change for each processing period). An example of the use of constant and variable data may be found in the processing of payrolls. Both constant and variable data are involved in the processing operation:

Constant data	Variable data
Employee's name	Total regular hours
Hourly wage rate	Total overtime hours
Number of dependents	Special contributions
Medical insurance	

Once a worker's name, identification number, hourly wage rate, number of declared dependents, medical insurance premiums, and other constant items have been recorded, it is unnecessary to insert these items again manually whenever a payroll is compiled. For example, if the payroll is processed from punched cards, the constant data previously mentioned could be punched into a "master" card. Once a master card has been prepared, several duplicates of it can be made. The prepunched duplicates can then be used whenever a payroll is to be processed. When a new payroll is to be compiled, a prepunched (duplicate) card for each employee containing that employee's constant data (name, number, deductions, etc.) is inserted in a card-punching machine. Because some of the employee's information has already been prepunched, only the variable data need be punched into the card. Because a considerable portion of the card has previously been punched and checked from a master card, the possibility of errors would be greatly reduced. If, however, any of the prepunched constant data were to change, such as the number of dependents claimed by the employee, it would be necessary to make an entire new set of prepunched (duplicate) cards from the individual's corrected master card and to destroy the outdated master and duplicate.

Better Information Provided

In addition to the major goal of reducing data processing costs, a goal of providing better information from the raw data must also be considered. *Better* information means better in terms of quantity and quality.

QUANTITY. The volume of data in terms of ability to handle the data no longer remains a major obstacle in most ADP systems. Equipment to store expanded volumes of data can usually be added to equipment already comprising the central processing system. For example, one processing center for a large banking operation in San Diego, California, has facilities to accommodate the records for its 300,000 customers; and the facilities may easily be expanded to care for 500,000 customers.

In these times of highly competitive business enterprises, faster processing of data and faster reporting of information are essential for management personnel to formulate effective policies and decisions. Even though the computational processes within a computer complex are expressed in terms of microseconds (millionths of a second), the input and output operations remain relatively slow. New equipment, however, is being developed to speed up slow input and output operations.

QUALITY. The second factor necessary for providing better information is that of quality of information. Quality not only pertains to the accuracy of data, but also to the versatility and flexibility of the processing. Dynamic business conditions require constant revision of the type of information needed. Simplicity of changing processing procedures is a necessity. The initial plan or system for processing the data in a specific operation will rarely be permanent but will have several revisions as time progresses. The changes in information requests by management will mean changes in processing sequences. One outstanding feature of the electronic computer is the facility for rapidly changing operational sequences without any adjustments of the equipment.

The goals of ADP may therefore be summarized as follows:

1. Reduce cost of information
   1.1 Reduce labor costs
   1.2 Reduce unit production costs
      1.21 Improve methods of reading and accepting initial data
      1.22 Eliminate intermediate processing steps
      1.23 Eliminate repetitive tasks
      1.24 Reduce handling of constant data

2. Provide better information for management
   2.1 Improve quantity
      2.11 Increase volume of pertinent information
      2.12 Increase speed of processing
   2.2 Improve quality
      2.21 Increase accuracy of information
      2.22 Provide flexibility in programs

REVIEW QUESTIONS

True–False

1. One obstacle in acquiring a basic knowledge of automated data processing is the lack of standardized definitions for data processing terms.
2. For an operation performed by a clerical worker to be classified as a part of a system, some preplanning of the operations must have previously occurred.
3. The modern concept of data processing includes several different operations performed during the processing of data.
4. All data appearing on the face of a source document should be punched into a punched card so that reference back to the source document will never have to be made at a future date.
5. All data punched into cards should be verified for 100 percent accuracy.

Multiple Choice

1. When a daily maximum temperature is recorded for each day of the month, and an average maximum monthly temperature is reported to a research organization

   a. The daily temperature would be classified as data.
   b. The daily temperature would be classified as information.
   c. The monthly average would be classified as data.
   d. The monthly average would be classified as information and the daily temperature would be classified as data.

2. An effective automated data processing system must include

   a. Processing data on expensive electronic equipment
   b. Performing tasks separately and ignoring other related tasks
   c. Repeating the same task many times
   d. Following operations exactly as used in some other successful business.

3. A preferable method to eliminate an inefficient office procedure would be to

    a. Increase the number of office personnel employed
    b. Replace old equipment with new equipment
    c. Devise a new system to make maximum use of equipment available in the office
    d. Redefine the goals and analyze the best procedures to achieve the goals in terms of personnel, procedures, and equipment.

4. The key words in defining integrated data processing operations are

    a. Electrified equipment
    b. Common languages
    c. Electronic computers
    d. Simplified operations.

5. A factor not usually considered in the reduction of data processing costs within a system is the

    a. Elimination of tasks frequently repeated in the office
    b. Reduction of the number of steps needed to reach a goal
    c. Use of smaller, cheaper equipment
    d. Use of consolidated records and reduction of handling constant data.

Classification

Classify the office machines listed below as IS&M, IDP, and EDP. Explain the reason for your classification.

Equipment	IS&M	IDP	EDP
Mimeograph			
Electric typewriter			
Carbon paper			
Punched-tape cash register			
Electronic computer			
Card punch			
Pegboard			
Desk calculator			
Microfilm			

Discussion

1. What is the difference between mechanized and automated operations?

2. What is the difference between the IDP and EDP classification?

3. How would the five manual steps in data processing cycles be applied to the sales slip for merchandise bought on credit?

Vocabulary ▬▬▬▬▬▬▬▬▬▬▬▬▬▬▬▬▬▬▬▬▬▬▬▬▬▬

Define the following terms in your own words:

IS&M	Automation	Mechanization	Input
IDP	Data	System	Output
EDP	Information	Source document	ADP

IS&M 2

INTERRELATIONSHIPS OF SYSTEMS AND MACHINES

INTRODUCTION

As noted earlier (p. 3), a *system* is concerned with a preplanned combination of procedures, personnel, and equipment which seeks to accomplish a prescribed goal. Every business operates on some type of system, good or bad as shown by its effectiveness in attaining a goal or objective. The manner in which a business operates or performs its tasks is the system in use for that business.

IS&M is concerned with the interrelationships of the system and the machines or devices involved. A business machine has changed from a piece of equipment performing one independent operation to a piece of equipment functioning as part of an overall objective or goal. Modern businesses must determine their objectives, plan an overall or integrated method of attaining the objectives, and specify the manner in which the tasks and routines are to be performed. This approach emphasizes the "system" behind the operation.

Although the IS&M category of automation seems relatively simple and insignificant, the correct use of machines and devices as related to a specific system is very important, and large operational savings can usually be realized through proper IS&M applications. When the proper machines or devices are correctly applied to business operations, we can expect to accomplish some of the following:

1. Elimination of repetitive writing
2. Elimination or reduction of human errors
3. Elimination of some paper handling
4. Reduction of human effort
5. Reduction of operating costs.

But businessmen must be aware of the machines and devices that can speed up the work flow through duplication, eliminate entry errors through "oneshot" recording methods, eliminate paper handling though "multipurpose" equipment, and reduce costs through task simplification and material savings. When businessmen make a thorough analysis of their problems, they often discover that additional equipment is not necessary; the system itself is lacking. Perhaps appropriate improvements in existing manual systems may be all that is needed. It is not always correct to assume that new equipment must be brought into the office and manual clerical operations be converted into mechanical operations. Mechanization and automation often receive the glory that could rightfully have gone to manual methods if those methods had been installed after careful analysis of the needs. Installation of new equipment may give a company status and prestige in its customers' eyes, but it may be a costly and unnecessary expense.

One primary factor involved in IS&M is that of data duplication. Small, simple data entries can often be eliminated through time-saving devices, such as the following:

1. Windowed envelopes (addresses need not be retyped)
2. Rubber stamps (arrival time and other data can be stamped on incoming correspondence; checks can be indorsed; specific instructions can be stamped on packages)
3. Gummed labels (return addresses can be placed on letters; requests for payment can be included with bills or invoices).

Large, complex data entries can often be eliminated by using one of the most common IS&M devices—carbon paper. Original recording is done manually only once (as illustrated in the following pegboard application), but the problem of creating the original entry still exists; data incorrectly entered on the original is duplicated along with the correct data.

PEGBOARDS

The pegboard, also known as a *writing board* or *accounting board*, is a rather simple device in which various sizes and shapes of forms are so placed over each other that an entry written on the top form will be reproduced in the correct columns on all the other forms under it through use of carbon paper. The backs of some forms may have "spots" of carbon placed on only those sections of the forms where duplication of entries is desired. The pegboard method does not require a large investment in machines or equipment, as only a metal "board" or plate with protruding pegs is used, but, specially designed forms for any particular operation must be purchased. Setting up a pegboard operation in a doctor's office for keeping patient accounts would probably cost, on the average, less than $150 for the board and the necessary printed forms.

One frequent application of pegboard accounting is in preparing company payrolls. Normally, the following three records are needed in a payroll operation:

1. A check to be given to the employee in the amount of the wage he has earned for that specific pay period

2. A compensation record for each employee that is kept by the company as a permanent record containing data on past and current pay periods

3. A check register (payroll journal) kept by the company listing all employees and amounts paid for one specific pay period.

The slow way to complete these three necessary reports would be to write each entry separately on the check, the compensation record, and the check register; three different entries would have to be made on three different forms.

If the payroll records must be manually written, one method of recording the entries could be a pegboard system similar to that illustrated here. In this system, only one entry (line number 1) need be written to make the necessary entries on the three required documents: the check, the employee compensation record, and the payroll journal.

The first (bottom) document anchored on the pegboard pegs, the large payroll journal (check register), is not moved during the recording of the payroll data. On top of the payroll journal is placed a sheet of carbon paper. On top of the carbon paper will be the employee's compensation record. This record is not actually placed over any of the pegs but is merely placed under the check to be written and against the pegs holding the other papers. The compensation records must be individually inserted and removed each time an employee's data is recorded. Note that the data previously recorded on this record is visible each time another check is processed; therefore, the constant data for each employee need only be copied from the lines visible above. The checks, the top documents, come in a group of overlapped checks. The top edge strip from which the check is later separated contains a carboned strip across it. As the data is written on the top check strip, it is duplicated onto the compensation record, and the carbon paper under the compensation record duplicates the data onto the payroll journal.

The following illustration shows an employee's compensation record inserted under the shingle of blank checks. When the payroll data for the employee is written on the strip at the top of the check, it is simultaneously recorded on his compensation record which has been inserted and also recorded on the next unused line of the payroll journal. After the payroll data has been recorded on the top strip, the actual check is written; no duplication of the check will occur because only the top strip of each check has been carboned.

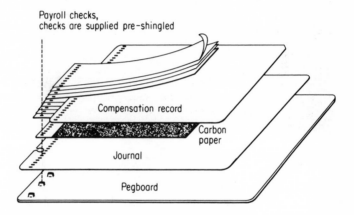

Payroll checks, checks are supplied pre-shingled

Compensation record

Carbon paper

Journal

Pegboard

From the illustrated payroll operation, we can see the following advantages of the pegboard device:

1. Copying of data is eliminated (the original entry is used on all required documents).

2. Proofreading is restricted to only one document.

3. Handling of forms is minimized.

4. Savings in time and space are realized.

KEYSORTING

The preceding description of an IS&M device, the pegboard, illustrates an economical system capable of reducing paper handling

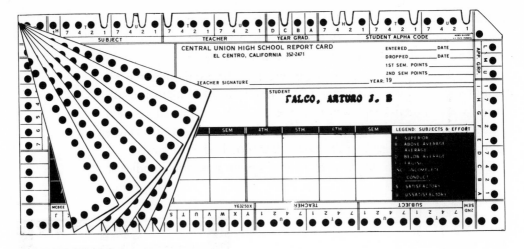

through simultaneous duplication by a very simple procedure using carbon paper. Another simple and inexpensive procedure applicable to sorting and classifying data is a device called a *keysort*. The keysort system can provide fast, accurate data processing without complex procedures, expensive equipment, or specially trained and technical personnel. The keysort system is used when records containing specific information must be selected from a large number of similar-sized records. Two elements are used in this sorting operation: (1) a notched card, (2) a keysorter.

The keysort card, which serves as a unit record and a source document, usually has holes located around all edges of the card. Although cards are available in many different sizes for different purposes, all cards used in any one specific application must be the same size, and all the holes appear in identical positions on each blank card. Certain sections of the card holes are assigned as "code fields" and contain information of a specific category. For example, certain groups of holes at the top of the keysort card illustrated contain coded data in the fields of the course subject, teacher, year in school, and student identification number. The code to be recorded is notched away so that there is no paper between the hole and the card edge. Numeric codes are the most prevalent type used in the keysort system. Once the keysort card has been properly notched, it becomes a mechanically sortable unit record to be sorted as desired.

Encoding the data into the cards by notching the edges can be done by hand notching devices or by machine notching devices. Hand notching is used when (1) the volume of cards to be notched is small, (2) notching speed is not a factor, (3) corrections are to be made. The most common device for hand notching is the key-sort hand notcher. If the same common notch need be placed in many cards, a "gang-notching" groover may be used to notch all required cards in one operation. Other notching equipment is avail-able, from a keysort keypunch to an electric keysort tabulating punch which notches cards, reads coded values already notched into cards, and prints summaries of the coded data notched into cards.

The keysorter is a long, steel needle set in a plastic handle; it

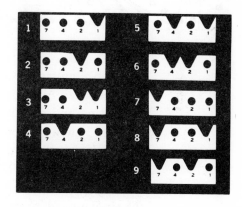

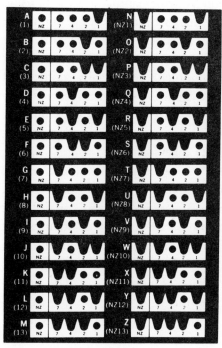

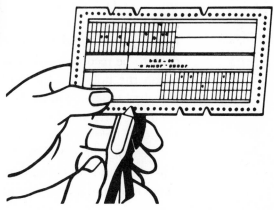

Keysort keypunch.

Keysort tabulating punch.

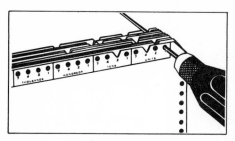

Keysorter inserted

Keysorting procedures

Keysorting procedures

Notched cards fall free

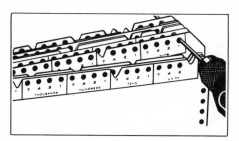

Keysorter raised

looks like an ice pick. The needle can easily be removed and another inserted, depending upon the length of needle required for the sorting operation. When the keysorter is inserted in one of the code positions of a group of cards, the notches allow the coded cards to be separated from the unnotched cards. Since the notched cards have nothing to support them on the keysorter, they fall free from the group, leaving the unnotched cards intact on the keysorter. By repeating this process for several notch positions within a code field, the keysorter can sort a group of cards into any desired order for a given code field.

Let's assume that a high school keeps student data on keysort cards. The code field for grade designation would contain four consecutive holes—the first for freshmen, the second for sophomores, the third for juniors, and the fourth for seniors. When a student's data has been originally recorded on a student card, one of the four holes in the code field is notched. If, during the school year, we want to know the names of all freshmen students, we would use the keysorter as follows:

1. Stack all student cards together so all holes are properly aligned.

2. Insert the keysorter (needle) through the hole identifying the freshmen code.

3. Raise the keysorter.

4. Remove all cards anchored to the keysorter. Those cards falling free from the keysorter will be the freshmen cards in which the hole has been notched away.

Thus we can see how, once the original data has been recorded and the keysort cards properly notched, this inexpensive device can reduce human searching and handling of records.

METAL PLATES

One clue to the desirability of adopting automated data processing devices is the frequency in which a specific office task is repeated. When a routine task is repeated over and over again, some systematic method of substituting mechanical operations for human operations is often beneficial in terms of a total system concept. One such concept is the use of metal plates.

The metal plate application involves *embossing*, recording data from raised type that has been punched into metal plates. Note in the illustration (p. 35) that the metal frame contains two inserts: on the bottom half of the frame is the metal plate previously punched on a special machine; on the top half of the frame is a paper card showing the content of the metal plate. The paper card is inserted to permit office personnel to read the contents of the plate held in the frame and thus make filing and plate handling easier. Filing and locating specific plates can be simplified by attaching metal tabs to the top of the frame. Tabs may be of different shapes and colors and may be attached at different locations along the top of the frames. Note in the illustration how the various tags placed on the frames distinguish one record from another.

A large number of codes may be applied to filing metal plates. For example, suppose a list of male students is needed. When student plates were filed alphabetically, a tag could have been attached to the top left of the frame for male students and the top right

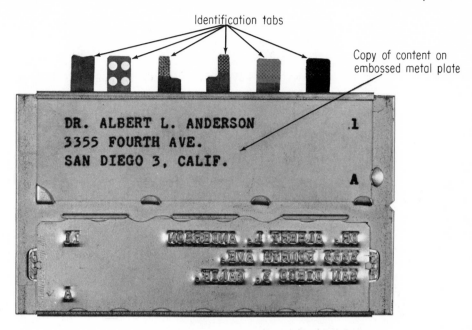

Identification tabs

Copy of content on embossed metal plate

Embossed metal plate

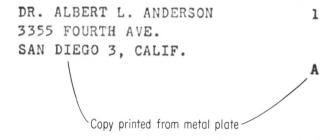

Copy printed from metal plate

Metal plate and printed copy.

for female students. As the plates are filed alphabetically, the tags make identification of the sex obvious.

Making the metal plates is simple. The embossing machine operates like an electric typewriter, but instead of a letter being printed when a key is depressed, a letter is stamped into a metal plate. The keyboard is also similar to that on a typewriter. After the plate has been stamped and released, it is anchored in the frame by metal clips and is then available for repetitive printing.

To print the embossed message on paper, the operator feeds the

Graphotype embossing machine.

desired plate into a printing position. An inked ribbon on the printing machine will be between the plate and the paper which is manually inserted. When the operator depresses an activating lever, a rubber platen rolls over the paper, thus pressing it on the embossed lettering imprinted on the metal plate. The platen then lifts, and the paper is removed with the letters printed on the

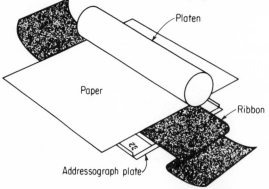

Courtesy of the Addressograph Multigraph Corporation.

Addressograph plate printing machine.

underside of the paper as it was inserted. A new plate may be automatically moved into print position as the former plate is ejected; or the same plate may remain in print position, depending upon the operator's control. For example, to print return addresses on many envelopes, the operator moves the desired return address into print position, properly inserts an envelope, face down, with the upper left corner directly above the metal plate. When the print lever is activated, the platen rolls across the envelope, and the embossed letters on the metal plate are printed. The platen raises, the envelope is removed, and a new envelope is inserted. The same address plate is used until the operator ejects it and calls for a different plate.

As may be seen in the illustration on p. 38, the plate may contain short messages as well as addresses.

Using metal plates for repetitious data has the following advantages:

Using metal plates to print short messages.

1. Data may be speedily and easily recorded.

2. Messages are legible, uniform, and neat.

3. Errors are eliminated once the metal plate has beeen correctly embossed.

4. Plate-making and plate-printing machines are simple to operate.

5. Files are easy to maintain, and plates are readily located.

MICROFILMING

Introduction

One major problem confronting businessmen today is control and retention of an ever-increasing volume of records. Most businessmen agree that huge volumes of records cannot be economically retained for long periods. One solution to this universal problem involves microfilming, a photographic process by which miniature copies of documents are recorded on film.

Microfilming was first used extensively in commercial banks, but successful applications have now been made wherever business records exist. Before the 1950's, microfilming was primarily used for dead storage; its purpose was to retain prior documents with the greatest possible conservation of space. Today, microfilms of all types of daily records are made and serve as an important communication media. Microfilming has changed from a simple application into a large, complex system involving many areas of specialization. Interest in microfilming increased rapidly after World War II when businessmen realized that future national disasters, such as atomic attacks, were possible. Original documents considered vital to a business must be adequately protected; a simple, accurate method of duplicating documents to permit one set of records to be stored in a safe, isolated area had to be found. Microfilming provided the answer.

Although many firms do keep records too long and spend excessive time and money on them, some records must be preserved and safeguarded because of federal and state laws. Normally, only essential documents should be microfilmed. The guidelines for microfilming are as follows:

1. When original documents cannot be retained by the business. (Example: canceled checks must be returned to persons writing them.)

2. When records are stored seven years or longer (example: case histories in hospitals).

3. When records are of permanent value (example: income tax returns, articles of incorporation, etc.).

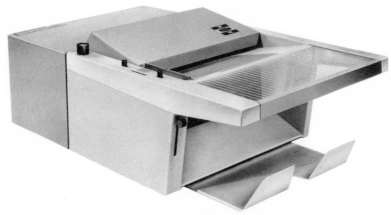

Microfilm camera.

Courtesy of the Remington Rand Office Systems Division of the Sperry Rand Corporation.

Record retention should be based upon future use for operational, legal, or historical purposes.

There is a vast array of microfilming equipment, including cameras, readers, printers, and mounters, manufactured by Remington Rand, Magnavox, Eastman Kodak, IBM, Bell and Howell, and many others. The types and sizes of microfilm also vary.

Standard- and legal-sized business letters and documents that may be frequently referred to are usually photographed on 16mm film. Documents seldom referred to may be photographed down one half of the width of the 16mm film and then up the other half as illustrated. The fronts of the documents may be photographed in

sequential order. The front followed by the back of each document may be presented.

The front and the back of each document may be simultaneously photographed and the images placed next to each other across the width of the film, as illustrated. Such an arrangement makes referencing easier by eliminating the chance of mistaking the back of one record for that of another. When considerable detail in small print appears on the original document, such as an engineer's blueprint or circuitry diagram, the larger 35mm film is used rather than the 8mm. The images then projected onto a viewer are larger and the detail more legible.

After the film is processed, the images may be kept on the film in the sequence in which they were photographed, or they may be separated and mounted individually or in groups. The images recorded on 35mm film are often mounted in punched cards and are called *aperture cards* (as discussed on pp. 85–88). Remington Rand

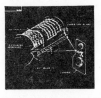

Uni-Kard jackets permit typed indexing information on the jacket to aid in filing. When images are to be classified by groups, Kard-a-Film jackets are available which contain openings in the plastic covers into which indexing strips and microfilm images may be inserted and removed.

Courtesy of the Remington Rand Office Systems Division of the Sperry Rand Corporation.

Microfilm reader-printer.

Courtesy of the Remington Rand Office Systems
Division of the Sperry Rand Corporation.

Microfilm file cabinet.

A variety of readers or viewers are available; some are capable of making copied prints of the images projected on to the viewing screen. Often the readers project the microfilm images on a larger-than-life-sized screen for easier reading and accommodate either 16mm or 35mm microfilm.

The film cabinet shown here may hold data on microfilm that would require 160 four-drawer regular file cabinets to hold in the form of the original documents. This film cabinet can store 900 rolls of 16mm microfilm or the equivalent of 3,000,000 letter-sized documents. Records are usually photographed on 100-foot reels of film—a reel may contain microfilm images of 13,000 blank checks, 5,800 three-by-five inch cards, or 3,000 business letters. The percentage of conventional filing space saved by microfilm applications normally ranges above 90 percent, with an average approximating

98 percent. The tremendous savings in office space is the advantage of microfilming which businessmen most commonly recognize.

But there are other advantages, too. Filing and retrieving information is fast and simple. After records are microfilmed, they remain in a fixed sequence with no chance of misfiling an individual record. Because modern equipment permits filming with a minimum of handling, the original documents remain in good condition without loss of legibility. When records must be transferred out of an office, perhaps from subsidiary to subsidiary or from home to branch offices, the microfilm system is an easy, rapid, and low-cost method of communication.

Microfilming offers decided advantages in preservation. Most microfilming is done on noncombustible acetate film. Reels may then be stored in fireproof containers. The film is more permanent than the finest quality paper (100 percent rag paper); and with proper care, the images will remain legible for 100 years and more.

In summary, the main advantages of microfilm are as follows:

1. Approximately 98 percent of conventional filing space is saved.

2. Microfilms may be conveniently stored in the main office area and need not be moved to distant storage rooms.

3. Any one image on a reel of film is in permanent sequence and cannot become disarranged or lost.

4. Noncombustible records can easily be stored in relatively small fire-resistant containers for protection against fire, theft, or other loss.

5. Duplicate copies with absolute accuracy may be made as enlarged prints from microfilmed images.

6. Large quantities of filed data can be cheaply transported over long distances.

Perhaps the main disadvantages of using microfilms are not confined to microfilming specifically but to all methods of copying documents—the tendency of businessmen to retain unnecessary documents, to make excessive copies of retained documents, and to resist the destruction of original documents after they have been microfilmed. Microfilming has three specific disadvantages:

1. Proper conditions of temperature, air circulation, and humidity must be maintained for storage. (Air-conditioned buildings have eliminated this disadvantage in many cases.)

2. Conversion to microfilm of large volumes of records stored before the adoption of microfilming procedures is costly and time-consuming.

3. Viewing unneeded documents is usually necessary in order to locate the desired document on a reel of microfilm.

REVIEW QUESTIONS

True–False

1. An office operating under an established system is operating in an efficient and effective manner.

2. Pegboard applications require the use of carbon paper (or carboned forms) and preprinted forms.

3. The basic principle applied to keysorting operations is the removal of unwanted records from desired records by having the unwanted records remain on the keysort needle during sorting operations.

4. Microfilm applications always store photographs of documents on reels of film.

5. Human errors will be eliminated when a pegboard device is used in a business system.

Multiple Choice

1. A key word used to describe IS&M applications is

   a. Electronics
   b. Computer
   c. Mechanical
   d. Integrated.

2. IS&M objectives are frequently accomplished through

    a. Reduction of paper handling
    b. Use of a computer
    c. Elimination of duplicate effort
    d. Reduction of paper handling and the elimination of duplicate effort
    e. Use of a computer and the elimination of duplicate effort.

3. Specific metal plates may be quickly located in files because

    a. Metal tabs identifying certain plates may be attached to the top of the plates.
    b. Information embossed on the plate may be quickly printed on paper.
    c. Embossed plates can be easily read.
    d. Only a limited number of plates are ever filed together.

4. An important advantage resulting from the use of microfilm is

    a. Information within a specific document may be rapidly obtained from microfilm reels.
    b. Film may be stored indefinitely without any air control requirements.
    c. Storage space is sharply reduced.
    d. Data can be extracted from film by direct inspection without the use of viewing equipment.

5. In any specific keysort operation,

    a. Keysort cards may be of various sizes.
    b. Constant information (same data) to be recorded in many cards must be recorded one card at a time.
    c. Cards must be hand notched.
    d. Cards may contain notches on all four edges.

Discussion

1. Is it necessary to have electronic equipment in a system which applies the following devices: keysort, microfilm, metal plates, pegboard?

2. What conditions within a business system would suggest the desirability of installing the processing media of keysorting, microfilming, pegboards, or metal plates?

3. What types and sizes of businesses would be able effectively to use keysorting, microfilming, pegboards, or metal plates?

Define the following terms in your own words:

Interrelationship	Keysorter	Metal plates
Integrate	Keysort card	Microfilm
Pegboard	Gang notching	Aperture card
Carbon stripping	Embossing	Film jacket

INTEGRATED DATA PROCESSING

INTRODUCTION

As noted earlier (p. 5), Integrated Data Processing concerns those procedures in which the source data is originally recorded in a common machine language that can be subsequently processed on various other machines. The distinguishing feature of the IDP classification is this common-language factor.

Since there are many different machine languages, the equipment to be used in any specific business operation must be able to read, interpret, and report through the selected language media. Each machine in the system must be able to communicate with the other machines; the machine language must be compatible. Because of this compatibility of machine language, IDP cannot be totally divorced from the IS&M concept—the overall system in which data are produced, manipulated, and reported remains a vital consideration in any ADP application.

It is impossible to cover all common languages in detail in this text. New machines utilizing different data processing concepts are being developed so rapidly that one could devote all his working hours to the single task of becoming familiar with new equipment developments. The office machine field is growing increasingly competitive; therefore, the quality, capability, function, and price of equipment are constantly changing.

The common-language media to be analyzed in this section include punched cards, punched tags and tickets, punched tapes, punched-edge cards, and photographic devices.

PUNCHED CARDS

Introduction

When an office executive wishes to "talk" to his secretary in terms of telling her what to typewrite in a letter, he dictates a letter into a tape recorder or some recording device capable of repeating his voice whenever the secretary wishes to play it back. The communicative media of the executive is his voice; in terms of recognizable sounds molded into English words, his voice serves as a common language which other people can understand. In automated data processing, the "voice" that commonly communicates with various types of automatic equipment is a series of holes punched into a card. This punched-card media has become the most universal and successful communicative media, or "voice," of data processing equipment.

The punched card is not a recent invention—the United States Census Bureau used punched cards on a limited basis in 1886. Of course, early uses of the cards are now considered very primitive. Today the usage of punched cards has become so common that most of us frequently encounter some application of punched cards. Bills mailed to customers by utilities, subscription notices sent by magazine publishers, and paychecks issued by large companies—these are but a few examples of our personal contacts with punched cards. Such contacts occur so often that the bill, subscription notice, or paychecks may not even be recognized as a punched card. The punches in the bill, subscription notice, or paycheck are meaningless to the persons paying the bill, returning the subscription notice, or cashing paychecks; those punches are the communicative media, or language, that will be interpreted by various data processing machines during processing operations, such as reading, printing, adding, subtracting, multiplying, dividing, classifying, and summarizing the data. The holes, then, represent the message.

Operation Principles

But how does a hole in a card become a "voice" or media capable of reporting facts and figures? If our data processing equipment can process punched cards, then that equipment must be capable of (1) recognizing the punches in a card, (2) determining where the punches are located in the card.

As the punched card enters and begins passing through the equipment, it passes over a small electrified metal cylinder. While the card passes over the cylinder which contains the electric charge, it also passes under small wire brushes capable of receiving an electric shock or impulse if and when the brushes come into contact with the electrified cylinder. As the card continues to move between the stationary roller and set of brushes, it serves as an insulator that prevents the electric current contained in the roller from reaching the wire brushes. As soon as the hole appears in the card as it passes through the equipment, the wires of the specific brush above the punched hole slip into the punched hole far enough to touch the electrified cylinder below the card and thus receive an electric shock or impulse. As we shall see later, this impulse is then translated into a letter or figure. As the card moves on, the wires of the brush are forced back on top of the card and are ready to drop down again into any other holes that may occur below the brush before the card completes the pass over the roller.

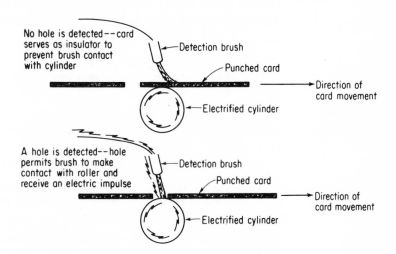

The hole in a punched card is similar in application to a hole in a roll of paper used on a player piano. When a hole in the piano roll passes by a certain activation rod, or "reading" mechanism, the hole permits air to be sucked into the mechanism at that specific spot and thus identifies what key on the piano keyboard is to be played. Similarly, like the player piano roll in which the position or location of holes designates what tune is to be played, the location of holes punched into a punched card designates what message is to be reported. But to understand how a punched card may contain a message, we must know what the various combinations of holes represent; we must know the code of the punches.

Punched Card Hollerith Code

Each punched card contains 80 vertical *columns* starting with column number 1 at the left edge of the card and going across the card to column number 80 at the right edge. The card also con-

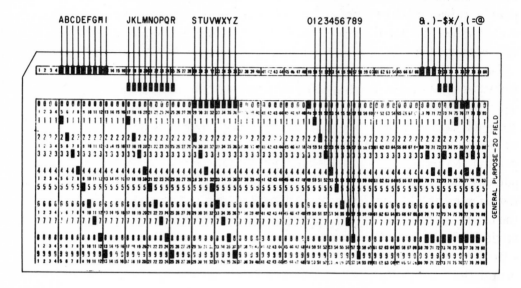

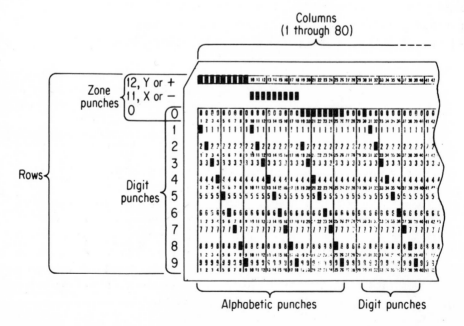

tains 12 horizontal *rows* from the top to the bottom of the card. The row across the top edge is called the 12-row and is sometimes referred to as the Y or the + (plus) row. The second row from the top is the 11-row, or the X or the − (minus) row. The third row down is the zero row. The rows below the zero row are assigned numbers beginning with 1 and ending with 9. Note that the rows of 0, 1, 2, 3, 4, 5, 6, 7, 8, and 9 correspond to the numbers printed on the card. A punch in any one of the rows will give the column in which it is punched the value of the row in which the punch was made. For example, a punch in a 5-row will represent a digit value of 5 for that specific column; a punch in the 8-row will represent a value of 8 for the column, etc.

The top three rows of the card—rows 12, 11, and zero—are also known as *zone rows* or *positions*. Actually, as shown in the preceding illustration, a punch in the zero row may represent either a zone or a digit value (a value of 0), but a punch in either the 12- or 11-row is always interpreted as a zone punch unless the ampersand (&) or minus (−) sign is intended. Zone punches are code punches that, when combined with a digit punch in any of the 1–9 rows, represent additional characters other than digits. As noted in the code card below, when a 12-row zone punch is punched into a vertical column that also contains a digit punch, the two punches —the 12-row zone punch and the digit punch—represent an alphabetic letter from A through I, depending upon the row in which the digit punch has been made. A zone punch in the 11-row along with a digit punch in any of the rows 1–9 will represent a letter from J through R; a zero zone punch along with a digit punch will

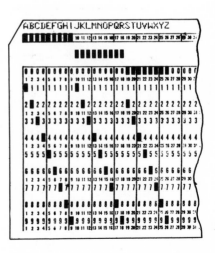

represent a letter from S through Z. Thus, to provide a code to represent the twenty-six letters in our alphabet, we must have a combination of one zone punch and one digit punch for each of the twenty-six letters.

The punched code for special characters and symbols, such as the &, $, *, @, and others, does not follow a systematic pattern, such as the code used to represent the letters in our alphabet. The combination of punches for special characters may or may not have a zone punch, may or may not have a digit punch, and may or may not require one, two, or three punches per column to designate the specific character.

We can summarize the coding for punching cards as follows:

Characters Printed	Number of Punches Required	Explanation
Numbers	One punch	Zero (0) value requires punch in zero row.
Alphabetic letters	Two punches One punch in a zone row One punch in a digit row	
Special characters	One, two, or three punches May be in digit rows and/or zone rows	Combination of punches not used to represent any other numeric or alphabetic characters.

Physical Characteristics of Cards

Because the punched cards often serve as communicative media among several data processing machines, it is important that the size of the cards be standardized for the specific machines that will process the cards. Generally, the cards are 7⅜ inches by 3¼ inches and 0.007 inches thick. Card lengths may vary from approximately 2½ inches to 16 inches for special purposes, but such cards require special processing equipment. To help insure accuracy during the processing of the cards, the paper quality must be sufficiently high to permit the machines to process the cards properly—cards cannot be torn or mutilated, and the edges cannot be curled or ragged. The quality of cards necessary to be used in any one specific operation depends upon the amount of use the cards will have; if they are to be used only once and then destroyed, the quality need not be as good as when the cards will serve as master cards and be used over and over again.

Some data processing machines require different methods of feeding or inserting the punched cards than others; almost all machines have the feeding instructions listed on them where the cards are to be inserted. Usually two specifications are listed: (1) which way the "face" must be; (2) which "edge" must be inserted first. *Face up* means that the side of the card containing the printing will be exposed or facing up after the card has been placed in the feeding mechanism. *Face down* means the printed side will be under the card with the blank side exposed. The "edge" of the card will be either the top of the card, the "12-edge" (the top row is the 12-row) or the bottom of the card, the "9-edge" (bottom row is the 9-row). For example, the directions describing how the cards are to be inserted into a processing machine might be read as illustrated—the cards must then be placed in the feeding mechanism with the 12-edge (top) going through the machine first; and they must be face up with the printing exposed.

Insert 12 row
face up

When a small section of one corner of the card is cut away, the corner cut permits visual inspection of a deck of cards to insure that all the cards are facing the same direction (printing is on the same side) and that all the cards have the same edge in the proper position. If the deck of cards has been dropped or some cards have been added or reinserted into the deck, any card out of position can easily be detected because its uncut corner will be exposed.

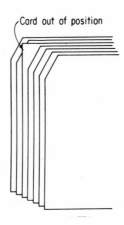

Card out of position

There is a trend toward rounding the three uncut corners. When the square corners become torn, folded, or dog-eared as the result of frequent handling, the damaged cards will not pass through the feeding mechanisms of the processing machines. Thus, rounded edges eliminate some processing problems because they are less susceptible to damage. Also, cards with rounded corners are easily inserted into envelopes and into card storage files.

Cut corner

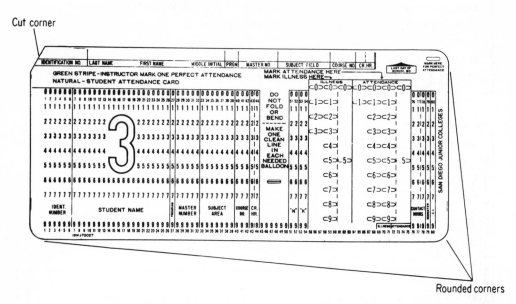

Rounded corners

In addition to size, weight, thickness, strength, moisture content, curl resistance, and other manufacturing specifications, cards may be purchased in a variety of colors. Most data processing cards used for general purposes are a "natural" or off-white shade, but cards are available in blue, brown, green, red, salmon, and yellow. Some businessmen prefer to use color-striped cards containing a ¼-inch colored stripe extending horizontally across the card at the top, bottom, or any preferred location. In some cases, several stripes of different colors may be used on the same card. Using colored or striped cards is merely a device to present an effective contrast for quick visual recognition of improperly placed cards.

Colored or striped cards cost somewhat more than the standard natural cards, but easy recognition may be worth the extra cost. Cards used for a specific purpose may be of one specific color—student attendance cards, for example, may be blue; grade cards, yellow; student identification or master cards, red, etc. When cards are frequently taken from their files or combined with other cards

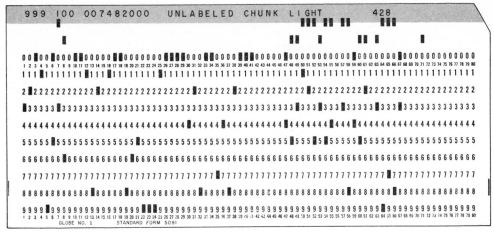

Striped card

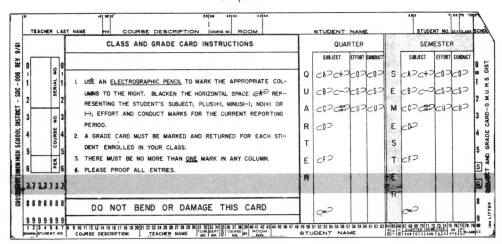

Striped card

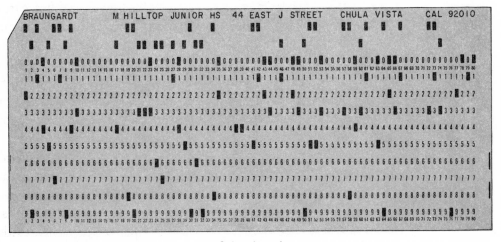

Colored card

to produce a specific report, cards erroneously refiled can be quickly detected when colored cards do not match the other cards in the file.

Card-punching Equipment

Several card punching machines are capable of transcribing our English letters, Arabic numbers, and symbols into the punched-card code. Two commonly used machines, called *keypunching machines,* are the IBM 24 Card Punch and the IBM 26 Printing Card Punch. The only difference between the two machines is that the IBM 26 prints the letters, numbers, and symbols above the 12-row at the top of the card as the holes are being punched. The IBM 24 does not print but only punches the code into the card. When the punched characters are also printed at the top of the card, someone who is not acquainted with the punch code can still read the contents punched into a card. A newer model of a card punch, the IBM 29, contains all the operating features of both the IBM 24 and the IBM 26 and has additional features to give even greater flexibility in punching operations. (Numbers are assigned to various data processing machines only to identify the machines in terms of their capacities and thus to eliminate the need to memorize technical names of equipment.)

IBM 24
(No printing)

IBM 26
(Contents printed)

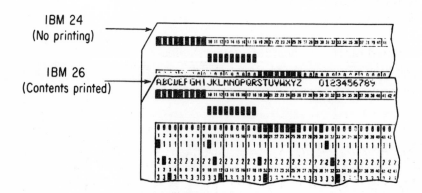

A card punch machine is operated quite similarly to an electric typewriter. Just as a character—letter, number, or symbol—is printed when a typist depresses a specific typewriter key, a character code is punched into a card when a card punch operator depresses a key on the card punch. Just as striking a key on the typewriter activates

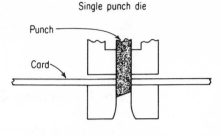

Single punch die

Punch

Card

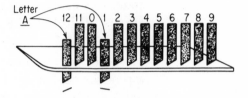

Punch dies punching letter A

Letter A   12 11 0 1 2 3 4 5 6 7 8 9

a type-bar which strikes the ribbon and prints on the paper, depressing a key on the card punch activates a cutting mechanism called a *punch die* which cuts the punch into a card.

The typewriter and card punch have the same lettered keyboard layouts; but there are two differences in the arrangements of the keyboards:

1. Because the card punch does not have lower case (small) letters, all letters are printed in upper case (capitals). The location of the alphabetic keys is the same on both the typewriter and the card punch.

2. As may be noted on the keyboard diagram, the location of the numeric keys on the card punch is not the same as the location of numeric keys on a typewriter keyboard. The

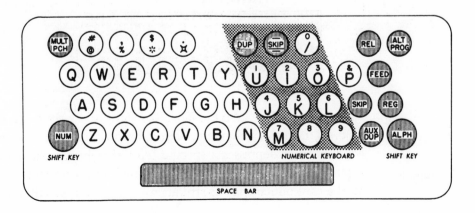

numeric keys are placed in the top row of the standard type-writer keyboard; the card punch groups the numeric keys in three different alphabetic rows and thus eliminates the difficult reaches and excess hand and arm movements used when striking numeric keys on a typewriter.

We shall discover later that most card punching involves punching of numeric data; therefore, the numeric keys are closely grouped in three rows to be operated by the right hand only and using a touch system similar but not identical to that used on 10-key adding and calculating machines. The three home-row fingers (the index, middle, and ring fingers) are placed on the keyboard letters of "J," "K," and "L" which contain the values of 4, 5, and 6, respectively. These three fingers go up one row for the values of 1, 2, and 3 and down one row for the values of 7, 8, and 9.

Courtesy of the IBM Corporation.

Alphabetic and numeric keyboard.

A shift operation similar to the shifting for capital letters on a typewriter is required when punching numbers on the card punch. No shift is necessary for alphabetic letters because all letters are always in upper case. We shall note later that the shift operations for punching numbers can be eliminated by automatic controls during the punching of cards.

When the data to be punched into the cards is to be all numeric, a numeric keyboard is available that does not have any alphabetic keys. No shifting is necessary when this type of card punch is used.

If an operator has previously acquired skill in typewriting, the time necessary to acquire skill in card punching will be substantially reduced. The actual punching of the cards is not difficult once the necessary machine adjustments have been made and the cards placed in the proper punching position.

Courtesy of the IBM Corporation.

Numeric keyboard.

Blank cards are placed in a card hopper (card storage bin) located at the upper right of the machine, as noted in the illustration. As the cards are needed, they move one at a time into a punching position directly under the punch dies. There are 12 punch dies in the punching unit; one die is positioned above each of the 12 rows on the card. As an operator depresses the desired key, one, two, or three punch dies will punch holes in the proper rows in a column to represent the code for that specific letter, number, or symbol. For example, when the "A" key is depressed on the keyboard, the die in the 12-row and the die in the 1-row will simultaneously punch the two holes necessary to represent the letter "A" in the card column.

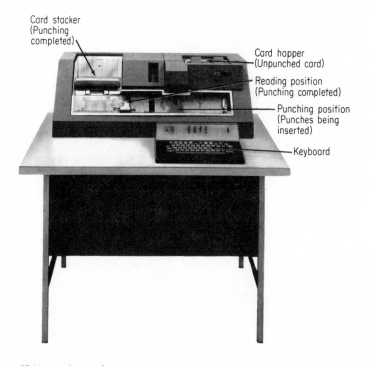

Card stacker
(Punching
completed)

Card hopper
(Unpunched card)

Reading position
(Punching completed)

Punching position
(Punches being
inserted)

Keyboard

Courtesy of the IBM Corporation.

IBM card punch.

The card then automatically moves one column forward to permit the dies for the next selected key to punch the proper holes in that column. Before the card has left the punching position and moved into the reading position, the card will have moved 80 times—one move for each of the 80 columns on the card—and the proper dies will have cut the necessary holes to represent the data to be recorded in the card's 80 columns.

Example of Card Punching Operations

Let's assume a card is to be punched containing the following data on an employee:

Payroll Data	Meaning of Data	Columns Where Punching Will Begin
8	Employee identification number	10
44	Total hours worked	19
500	Hourly wage rate	28
2600	Federal income tax withheld	37
950	Total other deductions	48
DOE JOHN J	Employee name	55

After a card has moved from the card hopper and has been fed into the punching position, Column 1 will be directly under the punching dies. Because the operator does not want to record any data until Column 10 has been reached (employee identification number), the operator will depress the space bar nine times until Column 10 is located directly under the punching dies. When the 8-key on the keyboard is depressed, a punch die will cut a hole in Row 8 of Column 10. The operator then spaces the card until Column 19 is in punching position. Then the number "4" is punched into Column 19; the card automatically moves to the next column (Column 20), and another "4" is punched into the card. After the card has been spaced to Column 28, the "5" is punched; then the "0" is punched in Column 29, and the second "0" will be punched in Column 30—the hourly wage rate of 500 has been recorded. Note that the dollar sign ($) and the decimal (.) in the data of $5.00 have not been entered; such symbols are implied and need not be punched. The operator spaces the card to Column 37 and then enters the income tax withheld ($26.00). Column 37 will contain the "2"; Column 38, the "6"; Column 39, a zero; and Column 40, a zero. Similarly, after the card has been spaced to Column

Punch dies punching number 8 in column 10

Number 8

12 11 0 1 2 3 4 5 6 7 8 9

Column 10

48, the $9.50 representing the total of other deductions will be punched into Columns 48, 49, and 50. The card will then be spaced to Column 55 where the first letter of the last name (the "D" in "DOE") will be punched. After the "D" has been punched in Column 55, the "O" in Column 56, the "E" in Column 57, and so on until the name has been recorded, the operator releases the completed card. The card then moves into "Reading Position" (see page 60 illustration). As the completed card leaves the punching position, another unpunched card automatically moves from the card hopper (storage bin) into punching position where the punching of data for our next employee will begin. The completed card for our first employee will appear as shown in the following illustration.

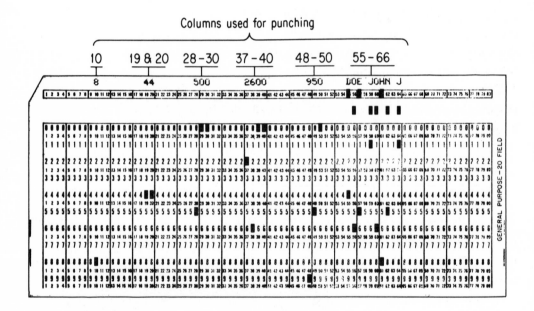

Note on the preceding card the following:

1. No punches appear in columns designating blanks.

2. One punch appears in columns containing a number (including zero).

3. Two punches appear in columns containing a letter.

This punched card for John J. Doe now contains a message in a common language—a language code that can be understood and interpreted by other machines that will be using this punched card. For example, a punch card calculator that accepts punched cards will read the data represented by the punched holes in the card and then do the calculations it has been preinstructed to do. In other words, the card provides the necessary data to processing machines for the computations just as a human operator provides the necessary data to a desk calculator by depressing the proper keys in the keyboard and selecting the proper function key, such as the add-, subtract-, multiply-, or divide-key on the keyboard of the calculator.

The punched holes, then, are the sources of data. When cards are run through a card sorter, for example, the sorter will analyze the punches in any specific column we wish to select. If a punch in the 1-row of that column is found by the sorter, the card will be sent to the storage bin or pocket used to hold all cards containing a "1" punch; a punch in the 2-row will tell the sorter to place the card in the "2" pocket. All twelve rows will be simultaneously checked by the sorter for punched holes in the specific column selected, and the cards will be sent to their respective pockets.

When punched cards are fed to a punched card printer, the printer checks for holes in the card. If a code has been punched in a column, that letter, number, or symbol represented by the punches

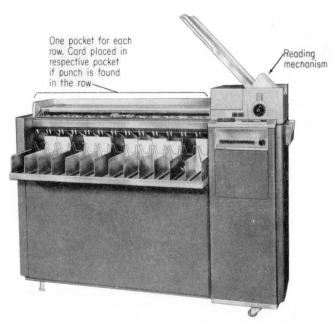

One pocket for each row. Card placed in respective pocket if punch is found in the row

Reading mechanism

Courtesy of the IBM Corporation.

Punched card sorter.

in the column will be printed on a tally-roll of paper in the printer. For example, each line of printing on the address labels illustrated represents the data punched into one punched card. Some of the addresses took three cards, some took four, and some took five cards. Again, the principle is similar to that of the player-piano. A hole in the piano roll caused a note to be played; a hole in the punched card caused a letter, number, or symbol to be printed.

```
MR. LESLEE A. ALLEN
19436 TROY PLACE
DETROIT 3, MICHIGAN


ARMSTRONG COLLEGE BOOKSTORE
LIBRARY
HAROLD WAY AT KITTREDGE STREET
BERKELEY, CALIFORNIA


MISS PANELA CAMPBELL, EDITOR
ICC BULLETIN
INTERNATIONAL COMPUTATION CENTER
PALAZZODEGLI, UFFICI, ZONADELL
ROME, ITALY
```

Data punched into cards is subdivided into groups of data representing specific types or subjects of information. These various groups of data are called *fields*. Notice in the payroll example (p. 61) that six different groups of data were given for each employee:

1. Employee identification number

2. Total hours worked

3. Hourly wage rate

4. Federal income tax withheld

5. Total other deductions

6. Employee name.

Each of these six specific types of data is called a field. These fields, or consecutive columns of data assigned to a specific category of data, are predetermined for each punched-card problem or application by the requirements of the processing steps in which the cards serve as the source of data for the data processing equipment. Although any number of the 80 card columns may be assigned for any specific field (from 1 to 80 columns for a field), the number of columns assigned must be adequate to accept the largest possible entry in that field when the data is punched into the card. For example, the first number in the previously mentioned payroll example for DOE JOHN J contained an employee identification number of only one digit, the number 8. Because the number 8 was punched into Column 10, nine preceding unused columns in the ten-digit field were also available. Thus the field could have contained any employee number from 1 (one digit) to 9,999,999,999 (ten digits).

Each designated field can contain one or more words. A *word* is any accepted combination of letters, numbers, or symbols. The first five fields of our payroll illustration contain only one word per field. These words are made up of one or more numbers. The last field

Field designation for payroll card

Employee number	Total hours worked	Hourly wage rate	Federal Income Tax Withheld	Total other deductions		Employee name
Field 1 10 digits	Field 2 10 digits	Field 3 10 digits	Field 4 10 digits	Field 5 10 digits		Field 6 26 digits
Col. 1-10	Col. 11-20	Col. 21-30	Col. 31-40	Col. 41-50		Col. 55-80

on the payroll card, the field containing the employee's name, contains as many words as necessary to record the proper name. "DOE JOHN J" is a three-word name within one field that will be punched into the card in our example. Actually, the number of words is not as important in allocating the number of card columns per specific field as is the total number of columns that may possibly be needed. In the payroll example, the first five fields that will contain numeric data were arbitrarily assigned ten columns for each field. The last field on the card begins at Column 55 and ends at Column 80—a total of 26 columns. Employees' names must be entered into the "Name of Employee" field so that the names will start at Column 55 and end on or before Column 80, the last available column in the field. The name may end in any column after Column 55; but it cannot contain more than the allotted 26 spaces and still fit into the designated field.

In practice, the assigned lengths of fields will vary from 1 to as many as 80 columns per field, depending upon the total possible spaces that may be needed to record the specific data. In our payroll example, only a limited amount of data was to be recorded on each employee's card; therefore, allocating columns for various fields was not a problem. If a large amount of data was to be punched into the cards, the first five fields of ten columns each could have been reduced considerably and still been adequate. For example, the ten columns allocated for Field 1 (Employee Identification Number) were not necessary; five columns would have provided space for 99,999 employees; four columns would cover 9,999 employees, and so on, depending upon the needs of the business. Field 2 (Total Hours Worked) would never exceed 99 hours per week; therefore, two columns would have been sufficient for it. Field 3 (Hourly Wage Rate) would never exceed four columns, or a possible $99.99; Field 4 (Federal Income Tax Withheld) would not exceed four columns or $99.99; and Field 5 (Total Other Deductions) would not exceed four columns or $99.99. Thus our card could have been designed as shown in the following table had it been necessary for us to conserve space on the card.

REVISED FORMAT FOR FIELD DESIGNATION

Field	Columns	
1	1– 5	Employee number—assume maximum of 99,999 employees.
2	6– 7	Total Hours worked—assume maximum of 99 per week.
3	8–11	Hourly wage rate—assume maximum of $99.99.

4	12–15	Federal income tax withheld—assume maximum of $99.99.
5	16–19	Total other deductions—assume maximum of $99.99.
6	20–45	Employee name—assume maximum of 26 letters.
	46–80	Blank—35 columns available for other data.

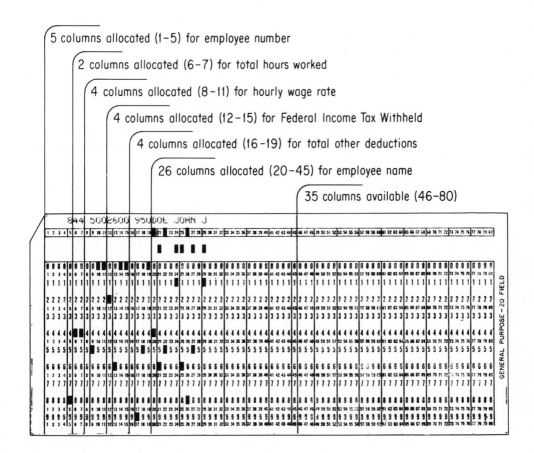

5 columns allocated (1–5) for employee number

2 columns allocated (6–7) for total hours worked

4 columns allocated (8–11) for hourly wage rate

4 columns allocated (12–15) for Federal Income Tax Withheld

4 columns allocated (16–19) for total other deductions

26 columns allocated (20–45) for employee name

35 columns available (46–80)

Once the fields have been determined and proved through trial runs, cards may be printed so that the fields can be labeled. Such a practice is very helpful to persons marking cards, punching data into cards, or reading the cards directly rather than reading a sheet of printed data made from the cards. Colored or striped cards (see p. 54) may be used to identify the purpose of that specific type of card. For example, in our payroll application a yellow card could have been a master card containing general information about our employee. A blue card might contain the payroll information necessary to compute his weekly pay. And a pink card could contain the earnings that he has accumulated during an assigned period of time.

GROSSMONT UNION HIGH SCHOOL DIST. SDC-008 REV. 7/63

STUDENT NAME (LAST—FIRST—MIDDLE) STUDENT NO | SCH | GRADE | PERIOD ENDING MO DAY YR | WITHDRAWAL

ACCUMULATIVE – ABSENCES – THIS MONTH
MARK SENSE THE TOTAL NUMBER OF DAYS ABSENT FOR THE APPROPRIATE REASON SHOW BELOW:

SCH. NO.	STUDENT NO.			WITHDRAWALS	NOT ENROLLED	ILL	NOT ILL	SUSPEN-SION	JUVENILE HALL	TRUANT	TOTAL DAYS NOT PRESENT

ABSENCE AND WITHDRAWAL CARD

REASON—MARK-SENSE—NOT ENROLLED

c1⊃ TO WORK

c2⊃ MARRIAGE

c3⊃ LACK OF INTEREST

c4⊃ MILITARY SERVICE

c5⊃ DISCIPLINARY

c6⊃ MOVED OUT OF DISTRICT

c7⊃ TRANSFERRED (WITHIN THE DISTRICT) TO:

c8⊃ OTHER—(SPECIFY)

1. WHEN REPORTING ABSENCE THE TOTAL DAYS NOT PRESENT AND THE APPROPRIATE REASONS WILL BE MARK-SENSED FOR THE SAME NUMBER OF DAYS.
2. WHEN REPORTING WITHDRAWALS, THE TOTAL DAYS NOT ENROLLED AND THE DAYS NOT ENROLLED WILL BE MARK SENSED ALONG WITH THE ⊂W⊃ AND REASON FOR WITHDRAWAL.
3. MORE THAN ONE CARD MAY BE USED DURING A MONTH FOR A STUDENTS TOTAL ABSENCES.

ILLNESS ABSENCES HAVE BEEN VERIFIED _____

WITHDRAWAL DATE __/__/__

(USE REVERSE SIDE IF NECESSARY)

STUDENT NAME

Mark sense columns (rows 0–9):
c0⊃ c0⊃ c0⊃ c0⊃ c0⊃ c0⊃ c0⊃ c0⊃ c0⊃
c1⊃ c1⊃ c1⊃ c1⊃ c1⊃ c1⊃ c1⊃ c1⊃ c1⊃
c2⊃ c2⊃ c2⊃ c2⊃ c2⊃ c2⊃ c2⊃ c2⊃ c2⊃
c3⊃ c3⊃ c3⊃ c3⊃ c3⊃ c3⊃ c3⊃ c3⊃ c3⊃
c4⊃ c4⊃ c4⊃ c4⊃ c4⊃ c4⊃ c4⊃ c4⊃ c4⊃
c5⊃ c5⊃ c5⊃ c5⊃ c5⊃ c5⊃ c5⊃ c5⊃ c5⊃
c6⊃ c6⊃ c6⊃ c6⊃ c6⊃ c6⊃ c6⊃ c6⊃ c6⊃
c7⊃ c7⊃ c7⊃ c7⊃ c7⊃ c7⊃ c7⊃ c7⊃ c7⊃
c8⊃ c8⊃ c8⊃ c8⊃ c8⊃ c8⊃ c8⊃ c8⊃ c8⊃
c9⊃ c9⊃ c9⊃ c9⊃ c9⊃ c9⊃ c9⊃ c9⊃ c9⊃

The preprinted card shown above is a card planned for the recording of school attendance. Note that each field has the description of that field printed on the card.

In our payroll example (pp. 62 and 65), note that when a field contains only numeric data, that numeric data is justified to the right of the field; the last digit is punched into the last column of the specific field. Data processing machines, like persons, must have proper alignment of the columns; when we add or subtract figures, we put all unit digits below each other, all tens, all hundreds, etc.; punching data into cards follows a similar alignment principle.

It is obvious now that the placement of data in the specifically assigned fields is highly important. So far in our discussion, we have placed the data in our payroll example in the proper locations by using the space bar on the keyboard to skip unused columns and

Justification of field data

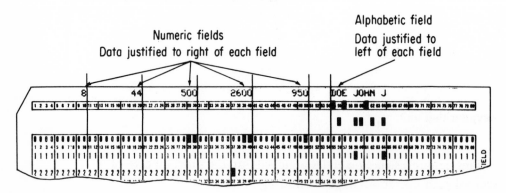

thus properly position the card before punching in the data for each field. There is, however, a much easier and more accurate method for positioning the card for punching.

Automated Punching Operations

The operation of the card punch machine can be additionally automated if part of the machine known as the *program unit* is used. Basically, the program unit consists of a prepunched card that instructs the card punch machine to perform specific operations. These operations are identified according to the holes punched into a separate card, called a *program card*. This card is not a data card and is never processed like one. On the popular IBM 24 and IBM 26 keypunching machines, normal programs could use the top four rows of the program card, the 12-, 11-, 0-, and 1-rows, to code the instructions.

Programming unit

Punching unit

Courtesy of the IBM Corporation.

Keypunching unit.

The various instruction codes punched into the program card can control such operations as the following:

1. Automatic shifting into either an all-lettered shift or an all-numbered shift; the keypunch operator need not manually depress the shift keys on the keyboard.

2. Automatic skipping over columns in the card that are to be left blank; the punch card operator need not manually depress the space bar on the keyboard. But the program card must contain the correct punches needed to define the beginning and the ending column of each field. When the machine gets the command from the program card to begin skipping, the skipping (spacing) will continue throughout the field until the machine gets another command from the program card to stop skipping. This automatic skipping operation is similar to the tabulation operation on a typewriter.

3. Automatic duplication of data previously punched into the columns of the preceding punched card may be performed on the card resting in the punching position; the key punch operator need not manually type in the data to be repeated. Punches in the program card must instruct what specific columns in the card being punched will contain the duplicate information from the preceding punched card.

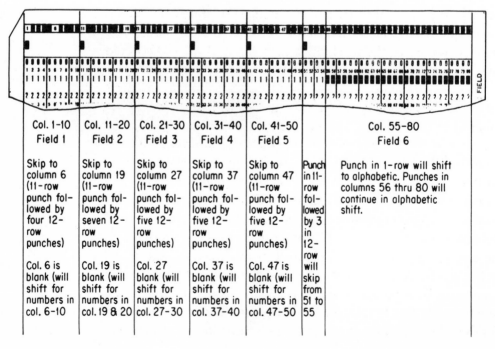

Col. 1–10	Col. 11–20	Col. 21–30	Col. 31–40	Col. 41–50		Col. 55–80
Field 1	Field 2	Field 3	Field 4	Field 5		Field 6
Skip to column 6 (11–row punch followed by four 12– row punches)	Skip to column 19 (11–row punch followed by seven 12– row punches)	Skip to column 27 (11–row punch followed by five 12– row punches)	Skip to column 37 (11–row punch followed by five 12– row punches)	Skip to column 47 (11–row punch followed by five 12– row punches)	Punch in 11– row fol– lowed by 3 in 12– row will skip from 51 to 55	Punch in 1–row will shift to alphabetic. Punches in columns 56 thru 80 will continue in alphabetic shift.
Col. 6 is blank (will shift for numbers in col. 6–10	Col. 19 is blank (will shift for numbers in col. 19 & 20	Col. 27 blank (will shift for numbers in col. 27–30	Col. 37 is blank (will shift for numbers in col. 37–40	Col. 47 is blank (will shift for numbers in col. 47–50		

Notice in the preceding illustration that a punch in the 11-row signifies the beginning of a skip operation that will continue as long as consecutive punches appear in the 12-row. Once a blank column is reached in the 12-row, the previous coded operation stops, and a new operation begins. For example, a punch in Column 1 in the 11-row signifies that a skipping operation will begin and will continue as long as there are following punches in the 12-row. The 12-row punches in Columns 2, 3, 4, and 5 will be interpreted by the machine to mean "continue the skipping operation." But as soon as a blank column appears in Row 12, the previously designated automatic operation stops. Thus a punch in the 11-row followed by a series of punches in the 12-row serves the same function during the punching of data into cards as the tabulation key on a typewriter.

After the card has reached Column 6 by the skipping operation, the card punch machine automatically shifts into a numeric position. This shift position is designated by an absence of a punch in the 1-row. The card will continue skipping operations whenever a punch is recognized in the 11-row and will stop skipping whenever a punch is found missing in the 12-row. But during the skipping and stopping operations, the machine is still in a numeric shift because no punch has been placed in Row 1. When, however, the card reaches Column 55, a punch does occur in the 1-row. This punch now implies that the machine is in alphabetic rather than in numeric shift. Whenever the machine is in alphabetic shift as a result of the program card, the operator must shift manually to punch in a number; whenever the machine is in numeric shift, the operator must manually shift to punch in a letter.

After the automatic operations needed in the punched card have been determined and a card punched to include them in the proper columns of the program card, the program card is wrapped around and secured to a metal cylinder called a *program drum*. The program drum is then placed in the program unit. A sensing device capable of determining what holes have been punched in the program card is then placed in contact with the program card. The program card moves one column at a time just as the card being punched moves one column at a time. The program card is synchronized with the card being punched—as Column 1 of the program card is read by the sensing device for instructions, Column 1 of the card being punched is in a punching position and is capable of receiving a punched code sent to it by the key being depressed by the operator. When Column 2 of the program card is sensed for specific instruc-

Program drum and card.

tions, the operator is punching data into Column 2 of the card in the punching position. The program card and the card being punched continue in synchronization until all 80 columns have been processed. Thus the program card with a pattern of punched holes symbolizing various automatic operations is wrapped around the program drum and inserted into the program unit, is examined by a sensing device, and initiates the mechanical operations designed to help the human operator complete the manual punching operations.

When many cards must be punched, the program unit will eliminate a considerable amount of time and human effort; but only when the cards to be punched contain the same defined fields can the program unit be beneficial. Provided that we do not change our field designations, each time we punch a card for one of our several thousand employees in the payroll example we shall not have to shift either to punch in numerical data or to punch in alphabetical data (employees' names); we need not hit the space bar to get into the proper punching columns—all of this will be done automatically by the program unit.

Remember that the more often a punched card is used in a data processing operation to produce the statements, reports, and other papers desired, the greater reason a business has for employing punched cards in its operation. Using punched cards depends to a large degree on the type and volume of information required of the business.

Design of Punched Cards

We have seen how using a program card can facilitate punching cards; we have noted the importance of keeping within defined fields when punching data into cards. The major task in card operations, therefore, is designing the card itself. With the wide variety of punched-card usage in many different types of business applications, the format or layout of the card needs to be carefully considered; the designated card must serve a specific function for which it has been designed and must be compatible with all equipment on which it is to be processed.

Here lies a major problem. How are the 80 available columns on a punched card to be allocated to the various groups of data (fields) that will be required to contain all the data that must be punched into all the cards to be used in a specific data processing operation? *What* data must be punched into the cards? *Where* will the data be located on the cards? Card design involves determining a pattern to be followed when the data is recorded in the cards. This necessitates a background knowledge of the situation, such as the accounting method used, the intended use of the data, the machines available to process the cards, the common or constant data that appears in the final documents, and many other factors. The cards will serve as the tool to provide the essential information needed by businessmen.

Before beginning to plan punched card designs, the various reports, statements, listings, and other papers to be used by businessmen are gathered and analyzed to determine what data appears on the various documents. If one is to use punched cards containing constant data, such as a person's name or identification number, his title, his department in which he works, or any other data that is seldom subject to change, this constant data may be prepunched

Punched card reproducer.

into the cards before the variable data is punched. Prepunching identical data into many cards in one operation is called *gang punching* and is done on a card reproducing machine, as shown in the illustration. After the cards have been gang-punched, they will be placed in the keypunching machine where the variable data will be punched into the cards one at a time.

Whatever documents are to be produced from cards and whatever cards must be used to produce the documents, it is still necessary to determine the number of card columns to be assigned each group of selected data that must be recorded in cards. The problem in designing a card is allocating sufficient but no extra columns to each field so as to receive the longest entry anticipated. If columns are allocated but never used, valuable card space is wasted.

How data is punched into cards may reduce the number of columns required. Some hints for reducing column requirements follow:

    1. Numeric codes can be used to replace English words. For example, the departments within a business may be punched as a numeric code:

Department Name	Department Code Number
Accounting	1
Sales	2
Shipping	3
Personnel	4

The number "1" punched into a card (only one column required) would mean "Accounting" to persons familiar with the code. Government records pertaining to social security benefits are maintained by a person's identification or "social security number" rather than by his name; but files are available where the name can be found by checking the cross reference of social security numbers.

2. Commonly accepted abbreviations are used whenever possible:

ST	Street	SR	Senior
AVE	Avenue	NY	New York
JR	Junior	CALIF	California
IBM	International Business Machines		
NCR	National Cash Register		

No periods are necessary following the abbreviations. Initials may be used for given names and may not have spaces between or periods following them:

> JD DOE   J SMITH JR

Commas are not necessary to separate city and state:

> CHICAGO ILL   ST LOUIS MO

3. If data to be punched into cards is to be taken from a specific source document, such as a sales order or invoice, the sequence of the data on cards should be similar to the sequence of the data on the source document. If the name is the first item read on the source document by the card

punch operator, then the name should be the first field which the operator will punch into the cards. It is easier and more accurate for a card punch operator to punch data into cards in the same sequence as it appears on, and is read from, the source document than it is for the operator to have to skip around on the source document to locate the desired data.

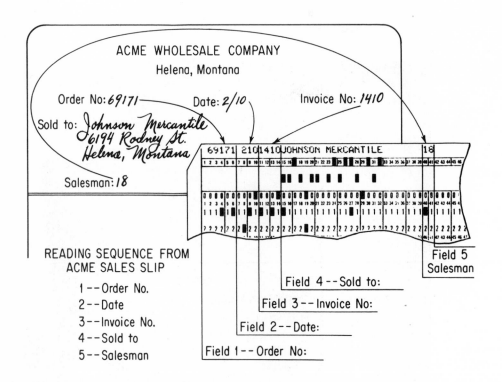

READING SEQUENCE FROM
ACME SALES SLIP

1 -- Order No.
2 -- Date
3 -- Invoice No.
4 -- Sold to
5 -- Salesman

Perhaps at this point we should note that the sequence in which the fields appear on a punched card need not be the sequence in which the fields appear on the sheet printed by a card printer. Through the facilities of the control-panel wiring within the printing equipment, the sequence of any specific columns can be changed as desired and extra columns can be inserted if additional blank spaces are desired. Many printers are capable of printing 120 columns (120 typewritten spaces) of data—40 columns more than the 80 columns available on the cards the printer reads to tell it what to print. By changing the position of certain wires on the control panel, extra columns can be added to serve as spaces; therefore, the practice of punching numbers into cards without intervening

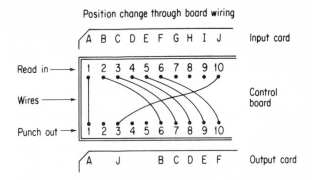

Position change through board wiring

A B C D E F G H I J   Input card

Read in →

1 2 3 4 5 6 7 8 9 10

Wires →   Control board

Punch out →

1 2 3 4 5 6 7 8 9 10

A   J   B C D E F   Output card

Printer control panel, showing wire connections.

columns for spaces is not a problem that arises when copy is produced on the printer. For example, the data presented from the sales slip in the preceding example would appear as follows on the punched card:

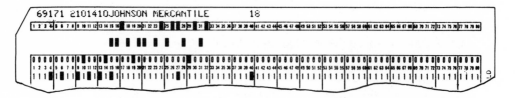

When this card is printed, data could be rearranged in any desired manner by changing the wiring on the control panel in the printer.

```
     69171  2101410JOHNSON MERCANTILE              18
●
  1410     18   JOHNSON MERCANTILE   69171        210                        ●
● 18    JOHNSON MERCANTILE           69171    210   1410                      ●
   JOHNSON MERCANTILE        69171     210      1410    18
●  69171     210      1410         JOHNSON MERCANTILE                      ● 18
```

In summary, the following points are to be remembered when designing a punched card:

1. Determine what data is necessary for the processing operation.

2. Allot enough columns for the longest conceivable entry for each field.

3. Minimize space requirements as much as possible.

4. Plan field sequence on the punch card in a sequence similar to that on the source document.

Punched Card Advantages

As a result of our previous discussion on punched cards, we can understand why punched cards have become so popular in data processing operations. Some previously noted advantages of punched-card operations are:

1. The cards serve as a storage media. A wide variety of storage applications using punched cards is available—aperture cards, mark-sensing cards, and others. (Some applications are discussed in detail on the following pages.)

2. The cards utilize a common language (punched code) that is comprehensible to man and is compatible for use in the majority of ADP equipment.

3. The cards serve as a permanent record. They contain written words and data just as any filed sheets of paper.

4. The cards are easily handled. They can be sorted and manipulated in a wide variety of operations. For example, filing operations are facilitated through the ease of searching for specific cards and data, maintaining and updating the files, and sorting the cards into desirable sequences.

5. The cards can be randomly selected when desired. Any card can be located without examining all the data on all the preceding cards (as is necessary in punched-tape and magnetic-tape operations).

6. The cards are physically adaptable to most operations. They are durable, easily replaced, and inexpensive (cost is approximately 0.1 cent, or one mill each).

7. The cards can be easily converted into other common-language media. The data from a card can be translated into punched tape or coded on to magnetic tape.

Punched Card Disadvantages

Some limiting factors in punched card operations are:

1. The cards are limited to only 80 columns of data. This limiting factor may require more than one card to contain the necessary information.

2. The cards are a comparatively slow media for equipment operations. The input or feeding of data and the output or printing of data is slower than punched tape and extremely slow when compared to magnetic tape.

3. The cards tend to become bulky as operations continue. A storage problem often results when large numbers of cards are processed and must be retained for future references. One reel of magnetic tape can store the same amount of data that would require punched cards stacked 18 stories high.

PUNCHED CARD PORT-A-PUNCH

Introduction

When "on-the-spot" card punching is required, the portable, lightweight, plastic, Port-a-Punch device is available. This pocket-sized punching device, which costs approximately $5, weighs less than one-half pound and can be comfortably held in one hand while the other hand does the punching.

To record data by punching the card, the person using the Port-a-Punch places the unpunched card in a plastic frame and on top of a rubber pad. A stylus, or metal-pointed pencil, is then used to push out the appropriate data in the correct rows and columns of the card. The punches are easily made as each number in the punching area on the card has been partially perforated when the card is manufactured.

This type of punching device is more frequently used when only a limited amount of data need be recorded, such as the record of school grades, the count of items in a merchandise inventory, the reading of statistical surveys or of gas and electricity meters. Constant data, such as names and addresses, is prepunched into the cards so that only the variable data need be punched with the Port-a-Punch which is merely an inexpensive device that permits direct entry of data into a punched card at the place where the data originates.

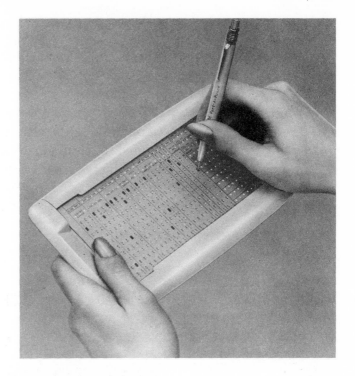

Courtesy of the IBM Corporation.

The use of Port-A-Punch cards and equipment.

Port-a-Punch Application

The Port-a-Punch card illustrated here is used to record utility meter readings. To the right of the card are six perforated columns: one column to record special information, such as a new meter, a meter leak, or a meter repair, and five columns to record the number read from the meter gauges. A card for each meter is prepunched with the customer's identification number, address, and other constant data. The cards are then sorted, and all cards pertaining to a designated route are given to an employee who will go to each of the meters listed on the cards and record the dial readings. At the

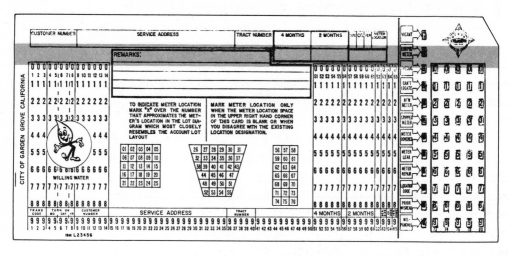

time the dials are read, the punches representing the readings are made into the card by using the Port-a-Punch stylus. When the cards are returned to the office at the end of the day, they can be processed immediately because the punches made by the meter reader need no additional interpretation; the numbers punched from the card are in the proper rows as designated in the Hollerith code previously discussed.

MARK-SENSED CARDS

Introduction

Closely related to the Port-a-Punch application is the mark-sense card. Both devices involve manual recording of data by methods

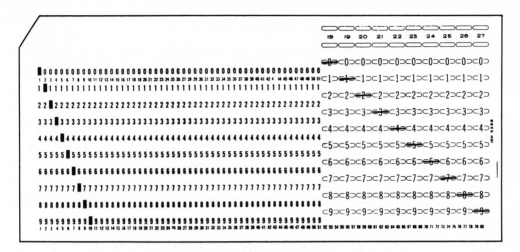

other than key punching machines. The Port-a-Punch actually records punched holes in a card. The mark-sensing device requires an additional operation to punch holes in the card after marks have been placed on it.

The cards containing marks are later fed to a mark-sense reader, called a *reproducer*, that converts the pencil marks into punches in the cards. The cards must be marked with lead containing a high graphite content that is electrically conductive. Actually, the method of reading the marks is quite simple. All blanks in which a mark may be placed are three card columns wide and are usually placed between the card rows so as not to interfere with punches that may occur in the same columns. Three sensing wires pass over a designated marking area, but only the middle wire sends out an electric impulse. The two outside wires are the receiving wires. If, for example, a blank has been filled in with a graphite mark, at the time of the reading an electric charge or impulse will be sent through the center wire and the graphite will transmit the impulse through the mark to the outside wires. If either or both of the outside wires receive an impulse, the mark-sense reader will know that a mark has been placed in that specific location. If no mark has been recorded, it will be impossible for either of the two receiving wires to record an impulse.

Like Port-a-Punch cards, mark-sense cards are usually prepunched with constant data; the variable data is entered at a later time. The mark-sensing device may be most efficiently used when the data is recorded at the place where the original data is found, such as at the locations of utility meters. Data is easily recorded, and persons marking the cards can continue to concentrate on their primary tasks with little attention diverted to data recording. Those persons marking the cards must, however, take care to record the proper marks in the correct columns and to do so with exactness so that the machines may later read and interpret the markings. Marks should be made with a single, strong stroke of the graphite pencil and should fill the mark blanks without extending beyond. Marks can, however, be carefully erased if erroneously recorded.

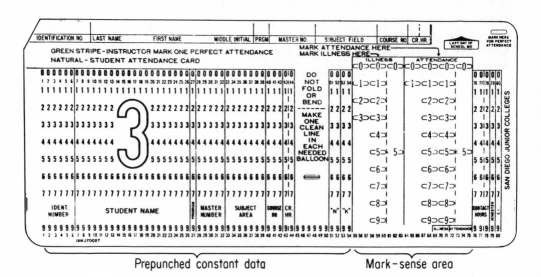

Prepunched constant data   Mark-sense area

Note that the attendance mark-sense card illustrated has the standard digit positions and is a regular punched card. Normally, mark-sense cards are designed so that the numeric rather than alphabetic data is marked. Alphabetic data, as you will recall, requires two punches and thus two marks per column and would require the marker to memorize the alphabetic code.

Mark-Sense Application

The mark-sense card illustrated is used to record student grades at the end of a quarter or semester. At the end of the grading period when the instructor is to submit the class grades, he is given one class card for each student in the class. A large portion of the card contains prepunched constant data about the student—name, identification number, teacher, and other information that can be recorded before the card is distributed to the instructor for mark-

Prepunched constant data

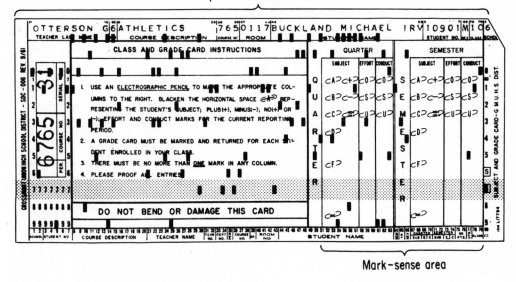

Mark-sense area

ing. The instructor will use a graphite pencil to record four marks: (1) the student's grade, (2) a grade qualifier (+, –, or neither), (3) his effort applied, (4) his conduct in class. As noted previously, mark-sense cards are usually used for recording digits rather than letters; the grade letters in this application will, however, assume numeric value for machine processing and will later be translated into a letter value for print-out.

After the cards are marked, the teacher returns them to the data processing facilities where the cards are fed to a mark-sense reader. The machine will read the marks electronically and punch in the proper holes in the proper columns. The punched card then becomes a unit record of a student's performance in a class.

APERTURE CARDS

Introduction

A newly developed field of automated data processing is IR—Information Retrieval. Because the production of records, forms, and reports has become so vast, the need to store and locate processed data has become increasingly important. One method of retrieving information is by using aperture cards. The function of the aperture card, also called Micro-Processed card, Filmsort card, and Micro-

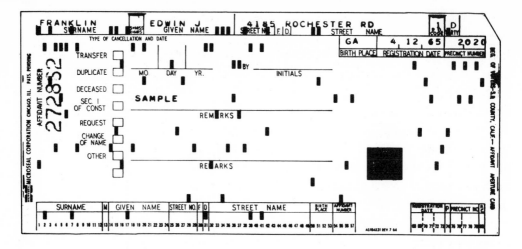

Data card, is to permit compact storage of information that may be easily located and interpreted by persons seeking specific information.

The voter registration card illustrated is a standard tabulating card in which a section of microfilm has been mounted. The recorded data printed along the top of the card and coded into the card with punched holes permits the card to serve as a unit record and enables its easy and rapid retrieval.

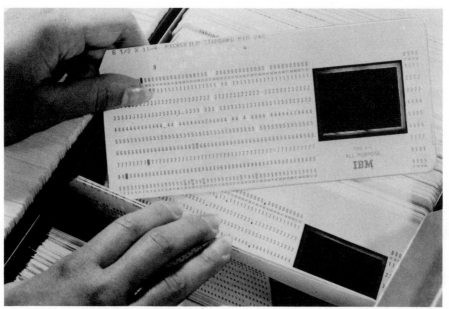

Courtesy of the IBM Corporation.

As shown in the illustration, the aperture cards can be compactly stored in the same manner as standard punched cards. Thus the information contained on large documents, such as construction blueprints, circuitry diagrams, or real estate plottings, may be reduced from huge, bulky, awkward source documents to small frames of film and inserted into a punched card.

After a specific aperture card has been located and pulled from the files, it may be inserted into a microviewer and printer which projects the contents of the aperture film onto a viewing screen up to 18 inches by 24 inches. Persons desiring the information may view the projected copy of the original source document. If a printed copy of the information projected on the viewing screen is desired, a paper copy up to 18 inches by 24 inches may be quickly made while the aperture card is in the microviewer and printer, and no reference need be made to the original document. Copies are frequently made when repairmen and servicemen must have the information away from the business office.

Storing data by aperture cards combines the following advantages of punched cards and of microfilms:

1. Filing space is reduced; savings automatically occur in equipment and facility costs.

2. Cards are easily handled and refiled. Standardized sizes permit use of punched card processing machines and card storage equipment.

3. Information can be retrieved faster. Searching is simple because the standardized cards may be electronically processed.

4. Original records are safer. Once photographed, original documents may be filed in security files, and referencing will be to aperture cards only.

5. Distribution of cards and transfer of information is a simple, efficient operation. Duplicate aperture cards are easily made and may be conveniently sent through the mails.

Aperture Card Application

A common application of aperture cards occurs in public utility companies where detailed records must be kept of all installations.

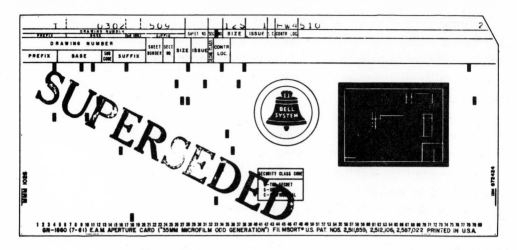

For example, a telephone company must not only know where telephones are placed, but must have a record of the circuitry or wiring of all installations. Because the blueprints or circuitry charts are so large and numerous, the company often uses aperture cards.

When telephones are installed, whether during original building construction or later, the circuitry charts are returned to the telephone company for filing. These original source documents are microfilmed and then placed in security files; additional referencing will then be made to the aperture card rather than the original chart. Information identifying the building, floor, room, and other pertinent data will then be punched into the cards containing the frames of the microfilm.

When later reference to the circuitry chart is necessary, for example, when a new telephone is to be added or the location of an existing telephone is to be changed, the aperture card pertaining to the specific room will be located and taken from the files. If only a check of the circuitry is needed, the film is merely projected onto the viewer; but if it is necessary for the servicemen to have a chart when they go to the installation, a printed copy of the microfilm is made from the viewer and given to them.

PUNCHED TAGS AND TICKETS

Introduction

Up to this point, we have discussed only those IDP systems associated with punched cards and using the Hollerith punch code.

The punched tag or ticket is a somewhat recent development in IDP which utilizes the same processing principle but a different punch code. Punched tags and tickets have found wide acceptance in merchandise retailing and inventory control. As stores increase in size and sales volume and as handling merchandise becomes more cumbersome, a faster method of pricing articles and keeping track of stock on hand is needed—a method in which electronic data processing can be applied.

Most persons have seen punched tags or tickets attached to garments, furniture, or other types of merchandise but have simply ignored their presence. The tags and tickets are small and are found in many shapes and sizes. The size used depends upon the type of merchandise to which the ticket will be attached and the amount of information to be encoded in it.

The tags or tickets are punched on punch-marker machines. These compact machines, about the size of a desk calculator, can produce up to 175 tags or tickets per minute and can perform any of the following operations during the making of the tags or tickets:

1. Codes compatible with code reading machines are punched into the tags or tickets.

2. Words and numbers corresponding to some of the punched codes are printed on the face of the tags or tickets.

3. Color striping (colormarking) may be placed across the tags and tickets to aid in classifying and routing after the tags and tickets have been removed from the merchandise.

Punch-marker machines may be manually or electrically operated. Specific keys on the top of the marker machine are set to the desired characters according to the information to be encoded into the tag or ticket. One tag or ticket is punched, with all punches made simultaneously. Then another tag or ticket moves into the punching position. If different data need to be recorded, new settings are made by moving the keys at the top of the marker machine.

After the tags or tickets have been punched, one or more of them are attached to the merchandise articles by pins, staples, string, adhesive, or button slots. When the merchandise is sold, the tags or tickets are removed. The use of the tags or tickets then varies according to business needs. Often the tags or tickets will be fed to a media reader which interprets the holes and transfers the punched data recorded in the tags or tickets to punched cards, punched tape, or a different media which is used to feed data into electronic computers. The computer will then compute the sales, update the inventory, print out reorder forms, and produce other desired reports and records. Writing sales tickets, counting merchandise items for inventory checks, checking items in stock—these manual operations may now be eliminated through the application of punched tags and tickets.

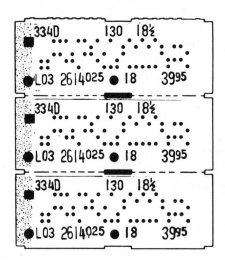

Punched Tag Application

As previously noted, large department stores frequently use automatic methods of processing data to obtain a more complete, accurate, and faster analysis of sales and merchandise control. The department store which employs the operation to be described switched to punched tags soon after it opened its first branch store and sales volume rose sharply.

When merchandise is received in the marking room, the invoices and purchase orders are carefully checked against the articles received to be certain that the received shipment is correct. When this verification is completed, the invoices are taken to the punching room where the tags are prepared. The tag puncher will get the necessary information from the invoice and set the keys on top of the punch marker. The information punched into the tags is illustrated. After the tags have been punched, they are attached to the various articles, and the merchandise in turn is sent to various departments.

Three identical tags are fastened to each article. When it is sold, two of the tags are torn away by the salesman for the following uses: (1) one tag for the accounting department, (2) one tag for the purchasing (inventory control) department. The third tag remains attached to the article so that the purchaser may have a purchase record to use for his own purposes or to return should he bring the article back for refund or exchange. On the back of each tag there appears the following printed message: "To be credited or exchanged

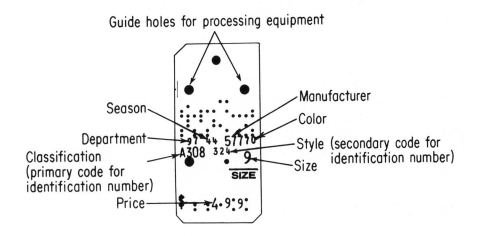

this article must be returned within seven days from the date of purchase WITH THIS TAG ATTACHED."

After the sale has been made and the two tags torn away, the tags are accumulated into two groups. At the end of the day's business, one group of removed tags is sent to a purchasing agency in another city; the other group goes to the accounting office. The accounting personnel will then feed the tags to a tag-to-card converter which will interpret the data punched in the input tags and produce as output a punched card containing similar information. This conversion to punched cards facilitates processing data on equipment designed to handle punched cards. The reproduced cards are then sent through a sorter in order to group them by departments, classifications, manufacturers, and style numbers. After the cards have been processed, daily reports are returned to finance managers, department managers, and merchandise managers. The punched cards are then stored and used at a later time to make periodic reports on a monthly or annual basis.

The numbering system used in punched tags and tickets is the same system used in most punched tape and magnetic tape applications and within the processing sections of electronic computers. The Hollerith code used in punched cards recorded one punch in one of the ten numeric rows to designate a specific number (see p. 50). The binary decimal system used in punched tags, punched tape, and magnetic tape is a different approach to coding numeric values.

BINARY-DECIMAL NUMBERING SYSTEM

Have you ever wondered why we count as we do? When we see the equation $5 + 2 = 7$ we understand what the "5," the "2," and the "7" mean in terms of recognizable quantities. But why? How have these symbols come to mean the things they do mean to us? Actually, about the only reason we can offer is that of custom: what was good enough for our forefathers is good enough for us. Numbering systems are like languages; we utilize the system of communicating ideas and thoughts through the symbols used by others in our own environment. When we look at symbols, such as MDCCLXXVI or 11011110000, we do not associate them with the year of our country's beginning as we do the symbol 1776. Yet MDCCLXXVI, 11011110000, and 1776 represent the same quantity.

We are used to a decimal numbering system based on ten digits (0–9) and placed in specific positions (units, tens, hundreds, thousands, etc.). Perhaps we would have been better off if the original planner of our 10-digit system had selected a 12-digit system because 12 can be subdivided by 5 digits to provide a more facile numbering base whereas our base of 10 can be subdivided by only 3 digits:

12-digit system		*10-digit system*	
$12 \div 1$			
$12 \div 2$	Five possible	$10 \div 1$	Three possible
$12 \div 3$	subdivisions	$10 \div 2$	subdivisions
$12 \div 4$		$10 \div 5$	
$12 \div 6$			

Whether our 10-digit decimal system was devised because man used his ten fingers or ten toes as counting aids is really unimpor-

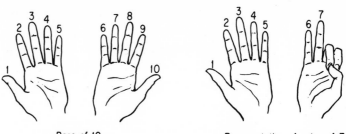

Base of 10   Representation of value of 7

tant; we know and understand this numbering system so it is the best system for us to use as a base when analyzing other numbering systems. And there are many other numbering systems. As a matter of fact, any number we wish to select could replace our "10" as a base. But man, with his ten fingers, can interpret any value represented by any one group of his ten fingers.

But electronic equipment used in data processing is only sufficiently intelligent to understand a numbering system based on two values instead of our customary ten values. It is much easier to represent only two possible numbers or symbols than it is to represent ten. When representing two values, either a symbol is absent (the value of 0) or the symbol is present (the value of 1). For example, if no hole is punched in a specific column on a card or tape, the value assigned to that specific column is zero; if a hole is punched, the column represents a value of one.

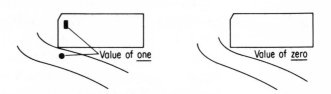

Value of one   Value of zero

Actually, the designers of our data processing equipment combined the use of binary representation (a numbering system with a base of two, as noted in the preceding paragraph) with our own decimal system (base of ten) to formulate a new counting system, the binary-decimal system. Instead of having each of our ten fingers represent a value of one more than the value assigned to the preceding finger, the designers decided to double the value of the preceding finger.

To help make the transition from decimal or human counting to binary or electronic counting, we must consider the element of position. In both our decimal system and the machine binary system, a starting point for any specific number must be determined and the

Binary numbering system

various values assigned to the left of the first selected position. In our system, we can assign any value from 0 through 9 to each position; in binary-decimal, only a 0 or a 1 value may be assigned.

	Decimal Positioning				*Binary-decimal Positioning*			
Millions	Thousands	Hundreds	Tens	Units	8	4	2	1
0	0	0	0	4	0	1	0	0
Decimal value = 4					Binary-decimal value = 4			

Note the importance of positioning numbers in both numbering systems. In the binary-decimal system, any decimal number may be formed by a combination of "1" values in the proper positions.

One method of representing the date of 1776 (see p. 92) was made up of the numbers 11011110000. From the illustration on p. 95, you can now understand the binary system of representing 1776.

Most devices used to represent binary data use only the first four columns or channels of figures (8, 4, 2, and 1) and use several rows to form numbers with values above 10, as shown in the following illustrations.

The illustration showing the value of 1776 represents a pure binary numbering system; as many positions as necessary are used to represent values identified to any specific number. The illustration of the punched tape shown on p. 95, however, represents the binary-decimal numbering system because only four positions are used for each digit; and the value of any specific number is determined by succeeding rows.

Note that the four channels on the left of the eight-channel tape are not used as number positions in the binary-decimal system.

Binary number positions

(Value doubled as it moves one position to left)

512 x 2	256 x 2	128 x 2	64 x 2	32 x 2	16 x 2	8 x 2	4 x 2	2 x 2	1 x 2	1
1024	512	256	128	64	32	16	8	4	2	1

1 = 1
= 2
1 = 3 (2 + 1)
= 4
1 = 5 (4 + 1)
= 6 (4 + 2)
1 = 7 (4+2+1)
= 8
1 = 9 (8 + 1)

= 44 (32+8+4)

= 147 (128+16+2+1)

= 1776 (1024+512+128+64+32+16)

11011110000

	Totals
1024	1024
512	512
0	0
128	128
64	64
32	32
16	16
0	0
0	0
0	0
0	0
	1776

Eight-column punched tape

Values

			8	4	2	1			
Row 1				●		●	5 Units	=	5
Row 2					●	●	3 Tens	=	30
Row 3			●			●	9 Hundreds	=	900
Row 4				●	●		6 Thousands	=	6000
									6935

Number to be recorded - - 6935

Only the four right channels (the 8-, 4-, 2-, and 1-channel) designate numeric values. As will be noted later, the other channels to the left are used for special codes, one of which contains a punch to designate the beginning or ending of one number and the start of another.

Eight-column punched tape   Numbers to be recorded: 715 and 6281

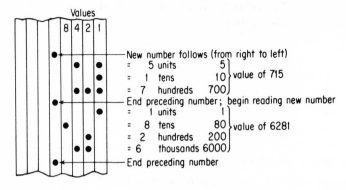

Data placed within a computer is often stored in the binary-decimal system as just described. When the data is moved from one part of the computer to another unit for manipulation and calculation, the mathematical processes are done in pure binary rather than binary-decimal. If the two figures mentioned were to be added together, the 715 and the 6281 would be taken from their binary-decimal storage form and changed to pure binary when transferred to the calculator. After the calculation, the answer of 6996 would be taken from the calculator and changed back into binary-decimal form for storage.

Binary Expansion

8192	4096	2048	1024	512	256	128	64	32	16	8	4	2	1	
0	0	0	0	1	0	1	1	0	0	1	0	1	1	= 715
0	1	1	0	0	0	1	0	0	0	1	0	0	1	= 6281

| Total | 0 | 1 | 1 | 0 | 1 | 1 | 0 | 1 | 0 | 1 | 0 | 1 | 0 | 0 | = 6996 |

carry one   carry one   carry one
carry one

$$512 + 128 + 64 + 8 + 2 + 1 = 715$$
$$4096 + 2048 + 128 + 8 + 1 = 6281$$
$$4096 + 2048 + 512 + 256 + 64 + 16 + 4 = 6996$$

It really is not necessary that we understand how the equipment handles and processes the binary-decimal numbers (we don't know how the rotary calculator selects and turns the various dials, yet we know how to use it). It is beneficial to know the basis of a binary-decimal numbering system and to remember the 8, 4, 2, 1 positioning. This binary numbering system and method of presentation is the basis of our machine (electronic) language, the language used by one machine to communicate with another.

PUNCHED TAPE

Introduction

Now that we have seen how a punched card can function as a media for a common language and how a numbering system based on the presence or absence of a punch can be interpreted, let's look more closely at the common language of punched tape. Basically, the underlying principle of punched tape is similar to that of punched cards in that a reading mechanism searches for and interprets recorded punches. There are two paramount differences between punched cards and punched tape:

1. A common language code different from the Hollerith punched card code is used in punched-tape operations.

2. A continuous record is produced in punched tape rather than the unit record punched into cards.

On May 24, 1844, Morse sent the first public telegraph message, "What Hath God Wrought," over a 40-mile wire between Washington and Baltimore. The importance of rapid communication became evident, and constant efforts in this field led to the origination of punched tape as a medium for transmitting coded messages across the land. Originally, transmission of codes represented in punched tape was done over metallic wire. Although wire is still used to communicate local messages, long-distance transmission of codes has been delegated to microwave radio.

Punched paper tape is becoming more and more important in modern data processing because it can be easily adapted to data processing equipment commonly used in business operations and offices. As noted earlier (p. o0) input functions in data processing are improved when input data can be directly transferred from a source document and recorded in a common-language media, such as punched cards, punched tape, etc. The punched codes can then be used as direct feed or input media for computer operations.

Courtesy of the National Cash Register Company.

NCR Sales-Tronic cash register and punched paper tape recorder.

For example, the accompanying illustration is a cash register commonly found in retail stores. A punched paper tape unit is attached to this cash register. After the details of the sales transaction have been set in the keys of the cash register, the activation bar on the register is depressed, and the transaction details are registered. When a punched tape unit is attached to the cash register, as shown in the illustration, the same details of the sales transaction are recorded automatically in the paper tape as a by-product of the cash register entry. At the end of a day's operation, the punched tape containing the details of all the recorded sales transactions for that day will be used as a direct input source for feeding the sales data to a computer. The computer then analyzes the sales data and provides businessmen with the data they are seeking. The illustration on p. 99 shows a desk-model bookkeeping machine that has a punched paper tape attachment. As entries are made on the bookkeeping machine, the details of the transactions are punched into the paper tape. Later the punched tape containing the daily postings of business transactions will be electronically read to a computer which will process the data. Many common business machines, such as cash registers, bookkeeping machines, adding

Courtesy of the National Cash Register Company.

Desk model bookkeeping machine and punched paper tape recorder.

machines, calculating machines, and typewriters, can easily be equipped with the punched paper tape recorder.

Punched paper tape has the following advantages:

1. Punched paper tape recording units can be easily and cheaply added to most common business machines.

2. By-product tapes produced by the punched tape recorders can be used as direct input for computer operations; the intermediary step of manually punching data from sales slips is eliminated.

3. Punch paper tapes are relatively cheap (approximately 25 cents per 100 feet).

4. Compared to punched cards, punched tape is more compact since more data can be recorded in the same amount of space.

5. Punched paper tape can be easily and cheaply mailed.

Punched paper tape does have some disadvantages:

1. Unit records from punched tape are not possible because data is continuously recorded; unlike punched cards, no specific space or columns are allotted in which data is recorded.

2. Data is recorded only as punched holes; no letters, numbers, or symbols for human reading can be printed on the tapes. If recorded data is to be proofread or interpreted by people, the codes must be machine interpreted and printed on paper.

3. Compared to magnetic tapes (discussed on pp. 114–116), both punched paper tape and punched cards are extremely slow media for feeding data to a computer.

AVAILABLE READING SPEEDS

(per second)

Punched tapes	1000 characters
Punched cards	1300 characters
Magnetic tape	340,000 characters
	680,000 numeric digits

4. Corrections and additions to recorded data are much more difficult to handle. Data on tapes are recorded serially (without any blank spaces). Individual punched cards with incorrect data can be withdrawn and replaced with correct cards.

Punched Tape Codes

The punched tapes first used to transmit telegraph messages over wires contained five channels into which the coded message could be recorded; most punched tape currently used in data processing and transmission consists of eight channels rather than five. As shown in the illustration, punched tape is available in either a five-, six-, seven-, or eight-channel tape. The eight-channel is becoming

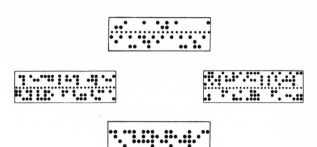

the most popular because additional channels permit a more sophisticated code with many built-in commands possible.

Data to be recorded is punched into the selected channels that run parallel along the length of the tape. Thus each row of punches across the tape contains a number, symbol, letter, or machine operation.

The eight channels are designated as follow:

Channels 1, 2, 4, and 8—a punch or combination of punches in these four channels represents numeric characters of 0–9 (see p. 95). The sum of the punched values indicates values other than the single-punch values of 1, 2, 4, and 8. Thus any digit from 0 through 9 can be represented by punches in four columns; ten rows were required for similar representation in punched cards.

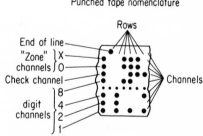

Punched tape nomenclature

Channel Check—this channel is used for mechanical checks only and does not concern us now. The punch, or "parity check" will be discussed later (p. 158).

Channels 0 and X—the "0" and "X" channels are used with the four numeric channels to record alphabetic characters and symbols. Thus these two channels serve the same function as zone rows in punched cards.

Channel EL—a punch in the "EL" or "end-of-line" channel represents the end of the line within a message and is similar to the carriage return on a typewriter.

8-channel punched paper tape code

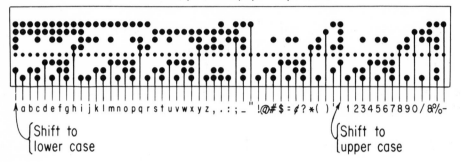

The eight channels in punched tape thus can register codes representing any letter, number, or symbol found on a typewriter keyboard. Note, however, one specific difference between the mechanical operation of the automatic typewriter that punches the preceding code and the regular manual or electric typewriter. When we depress the shift keys to get upper case (capital) letters on the manual or electric typewriter, that shift operation is in effect only as long as the finger keeps the shift key depressed; when the key is released, lower case (small) letters will again be printed. The automatic typewriter, however, retains the shift command in either upper or lower case, depending upon the last shift command it has received. Therefore, two shift keys are found on the automatic typewriter keyboard: one to punch or type in upper case and one to punch or type in lower case. Once the upper case shift key has been depressed, all the following characters will be recorded as though one had shifted for each letter on a manual or electric typewriter. To return to the regular or small letters, the lower case shift key must be depressed. Notice in the preceding illustration that all letters, numbers, and symbols through the percent sign were recorded when the shift was in lower case. The shift to upper case was then made and the remainder of the characters were recorded while the upper case shift was in effect. Note, too, that the punched codes for 1 2 3

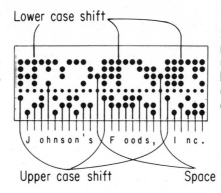

Lower case shift

Special codes needed to shift to upper or lower case but no spaces will appear in printout of copy

Code needed to type Johnson's Foods, Inc.

J ohnson's F oods, I nc.

Upper case shift   Space

4 5 6 7 8 9 0 / & % are the same punched codes used to represent ' @ # $ = ¢ ? * ( ) ; - but it is the shift code preceding these similar codes that designates which number or symbol will be printed.

For example, let's assume you wanted to punch into tape the following name: Johnson's Food, Inc. The following operations would be necessary on the automatic typewriter:

The carriage on the automatic typewriter, like the carriage on the manual or electric typewriter, may be tabulated to predetermined tab positions. If one or more tab settings must be passed before the carriage arrives at the desired tab setting, the automatic typewriter will read the tab code, move the carriage to the first tab stop, read the next tab code, move the carriage to the second tab stop, and so on, until the desired tab stop has been reached.

Another important code signal is the STOP code—a command for the automatic typewriter to stop its automatic operations as designated by a punch in the tape. Through this command, data other than that punched into the tape being processed can be manually typed by the typist. After the manual typing is completed and the typist wishes the automatic typewriter to continue typing from the punched tape, the typist will depress a "START READ" button on the automatic typewriter and the prepunched tape will then continue to control the typewriting.

Special operation codes

Carriage return

Feed holes for sprocket to guide tape movement in machines

Stop   Tabulation

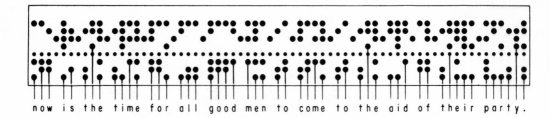

now is the time for all good men to come to the aid of their party.

From the code used in punched tape, as described on the preceding pages, we can see how the punches in a tape can produce a typed copy. Again, the comparison of coded messages in language to coded notes in a piano roll is applicable. Once the desired information is punched into our tape, the message contained in the tape may be reproduced as typed copy as many times as we wish to run the tape through the automatic typewriter and have the typewriter print out the message.

Basic Operations

The automatic typewriter can perform three basic operations:

1. Produce a manually typewritten copy in the same capacity as a standard or electric typewriter.

2. Produce a punched tape encoded with copy identical to that which was manually typed at the time the tape was being made.

3. Read a previously punched tape and reproduce copy as originally typed when the tape was being made.

Although the automatic typewriter can perform the functions of regular manual or electric typewriters and produce a manually typewritten copy, it is rarely so employed because that does not utilize the true capabilities of an automatic typewriter.

An important function of the automatic typewriter is the simultaneous production of a punched tape while the typist is producing a "hard copy"—a message typed on paper. The typewriter brings the unpunched paper tape into a punching mechanism which will punch the coded holes representing the key depressed on the keyboard. As the key is depressed and the letter, number, or symbol

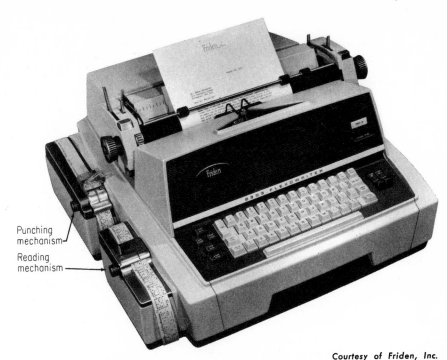

Punching
mechanism

Reading
mechanism

Punching and reading operations.

typed on the paper, the code is also punched into the tape, and the tape moves to the next position to receive the next punch. To punch the tape, the operator sets a "punch" switch to an "on" position, and the operator may begin the punching operation at any time.

After a tape has been punched, the tape can be read by loading it in the "read" mechanism and depressing the "TAPE READ" button. On this command, the codes punched into the tape will be interpreted by the reading mechanism; the keys representing the punched codes will be activated and the copy typed. If no manual entries are to be made in the letter, the entire letter will be automatically typed once the "TAPE READ" button has been depressed. Shifting, tabulating, spacing, and typewriting operations will all be done without human intervention; when the letter is completed, a "STOP" code will be read and the typewriting halted.

The illustrated letter is a form letter sent to selected participants in a survey study. After the message was punched into the tape on the automatic typewriter, the punched tape was used over and over again—the same tape instructed the typewriter how to type the message. Because only those letters were printed that were coded

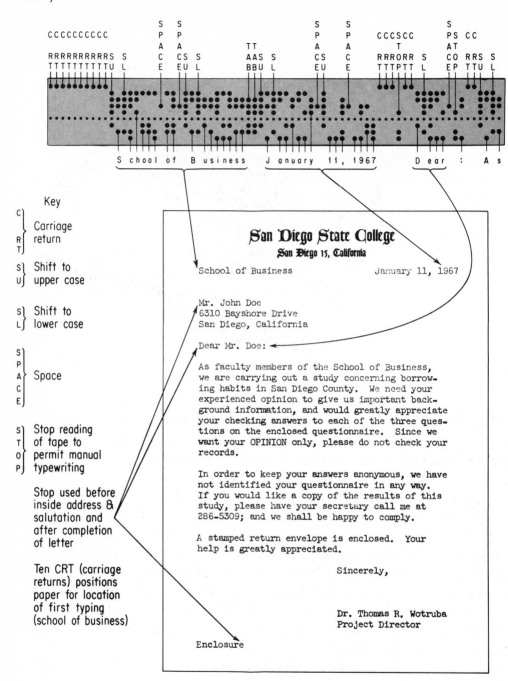

in the tape, all messages typed were errorless and each message was typed from tape at a rate of 120 words per minute.

When the stationery was inserted into the typewriter so that the top of the paper was even with the alignment scale (scale where the ribbon makes contact with the paper when a key is struck), the tape called for ten carriage returns so the first typewritten line would start on the tenth space from the top. Then the date was typed and three carriage returns completed; the typewriter then read a "STOP" code which halted the reading of the coded tape so that the typist could manually insert the inside address. After the typist had typed the address, the "TAPE READ" button was depressed; the carriage was returned twice; the word "Dear" was typed from tape; and the code "STOP" was again enforced. The typist then inserted the name of the addressee—"Mr. Doe" in our illustration—the "TAPE READ" button was depressed, and a colon was typed followed by the remainder of the message.

When the recipient of a lettter typed on an automatic typewriter looks at a completed letter, he probably assumes it was personally typewritten. During political campaigns, politicians frequently use automatic typewriters to contact voters and perhaps fool the voter into believing he has received a personal message from the person seeking office. When such letters are mailed to many homes, one typist may operate several automatic typewriters at once. Her only job will be to insert the address and salutation on a letter and then move to the next typewriter to repeat the same operation while the other typewriters are automatically completing the body of the letter from the punched tape. Of course, each machine must have its own tape; but letter production can be greatly increased with the automatic typewriter and the produced copy will be errorless.

Punched Tape Application—Telegrams

The process of transmitting messages has been significantly improved in recent years. But basic to the entire operation of telegram transmission is the punched paper tape through which the manual handling of telegrams is reduced to only one typing operation which is performed at the point of origin.

After the message to be sent is given to the operator at the originating station, the message is typed on a teletypewriter, a machine similar to a regular typewriter; like the automatic typewriter just discussed, it produces a punched tape as the message is typed. The coded tape containing the message is then passed through a transmitter which reads the coded message from the tape and relays it to a destination point. Selected codes in the tape that are interpreted at a message center permit automatic routing of the message to its destination.

The operator at the destination point edits the printed copy produced on the receiving set, and then puts the strip of paper containing the message on a telegram form before sending it to the person to whom the telegram was addressed.

EDGE-PUNCHED CARDS

Introduction

Another common-language media capable of reducing manual operations is edge-punched cards. The same code used in punched tape is used in edge-punched cards; the same reading mechanism on the automatic typewriter that reads punched tape can also read edge-punched cards. Many letters, invoices, insurance policies, and other documents typed on the automatic typewriter are products of both punched tape and edge-punched cards.

The primary advantage of using edge-punched cards is the ease of locating and handling prepunched data. Punched paper tape is somewhat cumbersome and bulky when filed as a roll and is difficult to handle when folded; edge-punched cards are of uniform size and thus easily filed and handled. If considerable data must be punched in an unbroken sequence, punched tape is used; if small bits of data (usually no longer than twenty words) are required, edge-punched cards are used. Examples of data punched into the cards are names of businesses or individuals, addresses, inventory items, or any short group of words which may be repeated on subsequent documents.

Application

The letter illustrated is the acknowledgment type of letter sometimes used by businesses to serve two purposes: (1) to inform the purchaser that his order has been received and is being processed, (2) to place the data pertaining to the order in a common-language media that may later be used to process the sale on electronic accounting machines. This preparation of data is done by punching a second tape which contains specific sections of the letter.

Only the dates, reference number, and quantity values on the

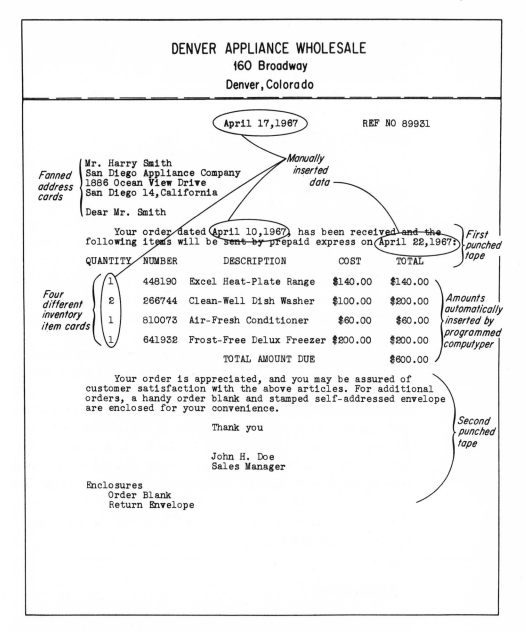

DENVER APPLIANCE WHOLESALE
160 Broadway
Denver, Colorado

April 17, 1967   REF NO 89931

Manually inserted data

Fanned address cards

Mr. Harry Smith
San Diego Appliance Company
1886 Ocean View Drive
San Diego 14, California

Dear Mr. Smith

    Your order dated April 10, 1967, has been received and the
following items will be sent by prepaid express on April 22, 1967:   *First punched tape*

QUANTITY	NUMBER	DESCRIPTION	COST	TOTAL
1	448190	Excel Heat-Plate Range	$140.00	$140.00
2	266744	Clean-Well Dish Washer	$100.00	$200.00
1	810073	Air-Fresh Conditioner	$60.00	$60.00
1	641932	Frost-Free Delux Freezer	$200.00	$200.00
		TOTAL AMOUNT DUE		$600.00

Four different inventory item cards

Amounts automatically inserted by programmed computyper

    Your order is appreciated, and you may be assured of
customer satisfaction with the above articles. For additional
orders, a handy order blank and stamped self-addressed envelope
are enclosed for your convenience.

        Thank you

        John H. Doe
        Sales Manager

Enclosures
    Order Blank
    Return Envelope

Second punched tape

illustrated letter would be manually typed; all other sections would
be typed from punched paper tape or edge-punched cards. The
manual typing would consist of the date of the letter (April 17,
1967), the date of the order (April 10, 1967), the date of the shipment (April 22, 1967), the reference number (89931), and the
quantities of each item to be sent. The first paragraph through the
title captions above the columns and the last paragraph including
the complimentary close, signature line, title line, and listed

enclosures, would be typed from two punched tapes—this constant data would be the same for all such letters. The variable sections of the letters (the recipient's address, the salutation, and each item to be listed) would be prepunched on edge-punched cards.

Let's follow through the preparation of the letter. The data and reference number are manually typed. Before the reference number of 98831 is typed, a switch is set which activates the punching of a second tape; as the number 98831 is typed in the letter, these five numbers are punched into the second tape. The tape-punching switch is now turned off, as no additional punching is needed until we arrive at the listing of the merchandise to be sent. The reference number identifies the purchaser rather than the name appearing in the inside address since it is easier to process by numbers than by alphabetic letters. After the reference number is typed, the fan of edge-punched cards shown in the illustration is inserted in the reading mechanism to type the inside address and salutation. Note that the first codes on the address cards tell the typewriter to return the carriage seven times—even the placement of the inside address is automatic. After the typing of the inside address and salutation is completed and a stop code is read, the operator inserts the first punched tape which, when activated, will read through the first three words (Your order dated), a stop code will halt the reading, the date (April 10, 1967) will be manually inserted, the activation key then starts the typing from the tape through the word "on" in the second line. A stop code permits manual entry of the date (April 22, 1967) and the activation key is again depressed so that the captions above the columns may be typed. The first punched tape has now been completed and is removed; however, no data from the tape has been punched into the second tape which, so far, contains only the reference number.

The operator then looks through her files of prepunched edge-punched cards containing inventory items and removes the card pertaining to the Excel Heat-Plate Range—inventory item number 448190. The card is removed from the files and loaded into the reading mechanism; the activation key is depressed. The carriage is automatically spaced to the proper position for entering the quantity, and a code to punch the next data into the second tape is read. When the operator types in the quantity of 1, the value of 1 is punched into the second tape. The activating (read) key is

Edge-punched cards

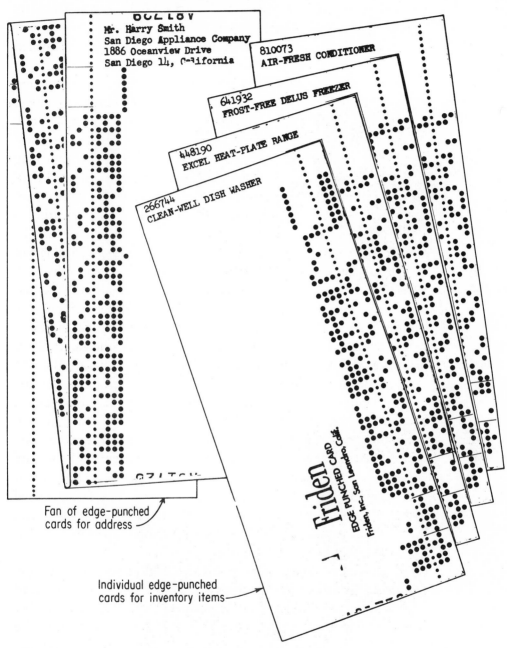

Fan of edge-punched
cards for address

Individual edge-punched
cards for inventory items

again depressed and the carriage spaces to the NUMBER position
where the number 448190 is typed automatically, and the number
is also punched into the second tape. The punching unit is then

shut off while the description of the item is automatically typed from the edge-punched card. The punching resumes when the cost figure is read from the card and typed on the copy.

Courtesy of Friden, Inc.

Friden 2201 Flexowriter automatic writing machine.

Courtesy of Friden, Inc.

Friden 5010 Computyper electronic billing and accounting machine.

At this point we should pause to mention that some automatic typewriters are capable not only of reading data from prepunched tapes and cards, but also of performing limited computations. The Computyper shown in the illustration is such a machine. In addition to the features of the automatic typewriter, the Computyper has a programming unit which performs the required computations at the selected locations in the letter. But the instructions for the computations must be programmed for each specific letter format; in our example, all letters have the same format so the programmed instructions would be changed when a new letter is written. When different jobs requiring different instructions are needed, the instruction (program) panel is easily removed and the proper panel inserted.

Thus, when the Computyper reaches the TOTAL column, the figures representing the value of the quantity (1) and the cost ($140.00) are multiplied and the product ($140.00) automatically typed in the TOTAL column and punched into the second tape. The next inventory item card is inserted, and the same process is repeated. After all the cards for the items ordered have been read, the second section of the punched tape is inserted. When the Computyper begins to read this second punched tape, it automatically moves to the proper tab setting to type in "TOTAL AMOUNT DUE." The instructions are followed to add the totals of each item, and the amount ($600.00) is typed on the letter and punched into the tape being made for later processing. If the automatic typewriter is used instead of the Computyper, the calculations must be manually figured and manually entered. In either case, after the total amount due has been entered, the remainder of the letter is then typed without interruption from the second tape.

The data processing tape being punched while certain sections of the letter are being typed now contains the reference number (the number of the account to be charged for the merchandise to be delivered), the quantities purchased, the item numbers, the costs of the items, the total extensions for each item, and the final total cost for all items ordered. When this by-product tape is given to a computer at a later date, the computer will process the data without additional human intervention.

This illustration shows how billing operations can be performed with a minimum of human effort. Accuracy is assured (assuming the prepunched tapes and edge-punched cards are correct), and paper handling is reduced to this one original operation.

MAGNETIC TAPES

Up to this point in our discussion of common languages we have reviewed some important factors pertaining to two frequently used media: punched cards and punched paper tape. We must become acquainted with another media, magnetic tape. Punched cards and punched paper tape are generally used for processing applications of small or intermediate volume; the magnetic tapes are used when a mass of data must be handled. Because large computer operations usually involve mass volumes of data to be processed at extremely rapid speeds, magnetic tapes are the most common media used for computers. Although the following chapter is devoted to electronic computers, magnetic tapes are discussed here because they are a common-language media which may also be used on data processing equipment other than computers.

The physical properties of magnetic tape used in data processing are quite similar to the properties of tape used on home audio tape recorders with a few notable exceptions:

1. The width of data processing tape may vary from ½ inch to 3 inches although the most common tapes are between ½ inch and 1 inch wide.

2. The length of tape per reel is usually from 1,200 to 3,000 feet, with 2,400 feet being a common length.

3. The quality of tape is much superior to that used on audio tape recorders.

But the recording of data on data processing equipment is similar to that on audio tape recorders. The tapes, which are about 2/100 of an inch thick (about the thickness of a human hair), are made of a plastic backing; one side is covered with iron oxide crystals which are capable of receiving and recording electric impulses. The data is read on and off the tapes by small read-write heads which

Low density magnetic tape copy

the tapes pass over. There is one distinct difference, however, between the recording of audio tapes and data processing tapes; the signals recorded on audio tapes are continuous, whereas the signals on data processing tapes are separated. The closeness of these separated signals is called the *density*.

Usually the density of recording is stated in the number of signals, called *bits*, per inch of tape. Up to 1,100 columns per inch may be recorded on super-high-density tape, but the most common densities are 200 (low-density) and 556 (high-density) columns per inch. The illustrated tape has been processed in a visi-mag solution to make the residual magnetic fields visible. Signals are invisible to the human eye on regular magnetic tape.

As shown in the illustration of the magnetic tape code, the code used to record data on magnetic tape represents a combination of the codes used in punched cards and in punched tape. The binary system (see p. 101) used for punched tape numerals and the use of zones for alphabetic data in punched cards are also used on magnetic tapes. We need not memorize the magnetic code as it is never seen on tape (unless chemically treated)—the code was presented merely to illustrate the similarity to other data codes.

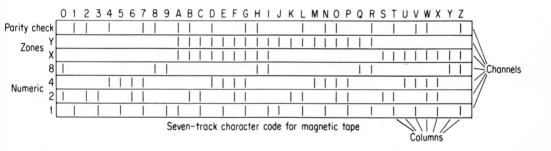

Seven-track character code for magnetic tape

An outstanding feature of magnetic tape is the speed at which data may be read and recorded. Speeds may range up to 150 inches per second. If the 150 inches of tape passing over the read-write heads had a density of 1,100 digits per inch, the data may be read or written at a rate of 165,000 characters per second. No other means of recording machine language can compare with this rate of speed.

Another prime advantage of magnetic tape is the high density in which an extremely large amount of data can be stored. One reel of the commonly used high-density tape can contain the same amount of data as that recorded in 180,000 punched cards filed away in three punched card filing cabinets. Of course, the super-high-density magnetic tape could contain twice the amount of data, or the equivalent of 360,000 punched cards. With improvements in the manufacture of magnetic tape constantly being made, the density figures per inch are going higher and higher.

To function properly in data processing equipment, magnetic tape must be carefully handled and stored. Because any foreign particles on a tape may be erroneously interpreted by a read-write head as a stored bit, the tapes are often kept in air-conditioned rooms in which clean air is maintained at specified temperature and humidity levels.

A second disadvantage of magnetic tape is the need for careful handling when the tape is threaded on the processing equipment. The oil from human skin or any creases in the tape may give an incorrect reading, since the bits are extremely tiny and closely spaced.

In spite of some disadvantages in employing magnetic tape, we shall undoubtedly see substantial increase in the use of this media in the future because of its outstanding features of speed and density.

REVIEW QUESTIONS

True–False

1. The "zero" row in punched cards serves as a zone punch and a digit punch.

2. The systematic punched code used in punched paper tapes should be memorized by persons who operate punched-tape equipment.

3. During any specific punched card operation, all cards must be of the same size, color, corner cut, weight, and thickness.

4. The keyboard layout of the IBM 26 and IBM 29 card punch is identical to the keyboard layout of a standard or electric typewriter.

5. A punch-card data field may not contain more than one word or set of digits.

6. Once the number of spaces has been assigned to a card field and cards are made ready for punching, the length of the fields cannot be expanded during punching operations to include additional card columns.

7. Binary numbering systems are used in data processing more as a media adaptable in machine construction than as a media to be interpreted by humans.

8. Port-a-Punch cards are processed in the same manner and in similar sequence as mark-sense cards.

9. Fields in punched tape applications must be rigidly defined and cannot vary in length when tapes are being punched.

10. The code used to store data on magnetic tape is similar to the punched paper tape code.

Multiple Choice

1. A key word used to describe IDP applications is

   a. Common language
   b. Computers
   c. Punched cards
   d. Binary decimal.

2. A storage media used in data processing which differs from the majority of media listed below in terms of the mechanical method of storing data is

   a. Punched cards
   b. Paper tape
   c. Magnetic tape
   d. Edge-punched cards.

3. The code used in punched cards is called the

   a. IBM code
   b. Binary code
   c. Hollerith code
   d. Punched card code.

4. If the number "754" is to be punched in a card field starting at Column 11 and ending with Column 20, the "7" would be punched in

   a. Column 11
   b. Column 14
   c. Column 16
   d. Column 18.

5. If the name DOE is to be punched in a card field starting at

Column 11 and ending with Column 20, the "D" would be punched in

a. Column 11
b. Column 14
c. Column 16
d. Column 18.

6. The automatic operations controlled by a program card include

a. Skipping columns
b. Skipping columns and shifting
c. Skipping columns, shifting, and duplicating
d. Skipping columns, shifting, duplicating, and verifying.

7. If you were given a completed set of manually addressed envelopes and asked to punch a card containing the data in each address, the first field you would punch into a card would be the

a. Name
b. Street address
c. City
d. State.

8. The binary number of 0110 would have a decimal value of

a. 2
b. 4
c. 5
d. 6.

9. Automatic typewriters would be more appropriately used in a data processing system which

a. Repeated the same data in each output document
b. Required extremely rapid output printing
c. Contained considerable variable data in each output document
d. Totally eliminated the need for human operations.

10. One disadvantage in the use of magnetic tape is its

a. Slow speed
b. Limited storage capacity
c. Outdated application in modern equipment
d. Handling and storage problems.

Discussion

1. What is the difference between the binary and the binary-decimal numbering system?

2. What are the advantages and disadvantages in the use of Port-a-Punch cards, mark-sense cards, standard punched cards, punched paper tape, and magnetic tape?

3. What types of business could make use of the processing media of Port-a-Punch cards, mark-sense cards, standard punched cards, and automatic typewriters?

Vocabulary

Define the following terms in your own words:

IDP	IBM 29	Program card
Common language	Keypunch	Port-a-Punch
Hollerith code	Tabulating machines	Mark-sense
Card column	Punch die	Aperture card
Card row	Card read position	Punched tag/ticket
Zone row	Card punch position	Binary
Card 12 edge	Word	Binary-decimal
Card 9 edge	Field	Automatic typewriter
IBM 24	Programming unit	Computyper
IBM 26	Program drum	Edge-punched card
		Magnetic tape

Punched-card Design Problem

Design a punched card to contain the data needed to produce a student's grade report. The report, which is to be mailed in a windowed envelope and addressed to the student, will be distributed at the end of each six-week period. The copy sent to the student must be signed by the student's parent or guardian and returned to the student's homeroom teacher. This procedure for distributing grades is expected to remain unchanged for an additional ten years.

The grade report will appear as shown on page 120.

The listing of grades will be taken from class cards. Six cards will be needed, including one card for each of the six periods comprising the school day. (Study hall will also be listed but no grade will be assigned in the "GRADE" column.) Another card indicating the grading period and date will also be included. The sequence in which the cards will be inserted into the printer to produce the foregoing grade report will be as follows:

1. Master card (containing the constant data—the card you are to design for this problem)

2. Class cards (six cards containing data for each of the six class periods)

3. Variable card (containing the grading period and date).

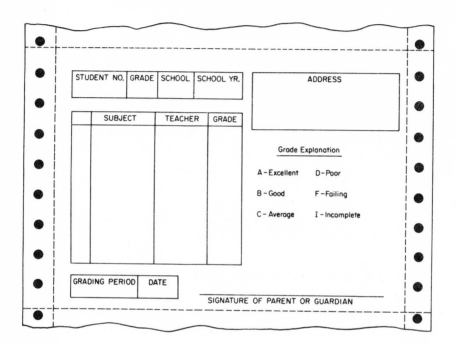

The card you are designing must contain the constant data to be used each time the grade report is printed during this school year; therefore, only the data that will not change should appear on this card.

The following factors must be considered:

1. There are seven high schools in the school district—all data processing of reports, such as the grade report illustrated on the preceding page, will be done in the district office rather than in each high school.

2. The largest number currently assigned to a student is 96,814—at least 5,000 additional students are expected in the next school year (numbers are assigned consecutively from 96,814).

3. Each fall new cards are made from the cards currently being used as the constant or master card. Any changes in the card, such as the "grade" and "school year," will be made by the operator who punches in the data from the previous constant card.

Procedure:

1. Determine in what sequence the data should be punched into the cards.

   Format of the card should be designed so that the sequence in which data is read from the previous year's card will be the same sequence in which data is being punched.

2. Determine how many columns should be allotted for each of the five fields.

   Use only the last two digits in the year (the "19" is not necessary) and separate the two years with a hyphen (no spaces are needed before or after the hyphen).

   Use only the initials for the given name (first name) and the middle name, but spell the surname (last name) in full.

   Determine how many lines are necessary in the mailing addresses and how many columns can be allotted for each line.

   Remember, you have only 80 columns—plan to allot all of them.

   Allot the number of columns necessary for numeric columns, then determine how many columns are left for alphabetic data (addresses).

   Do not allot more columns than will be necessary to contain the longest data in any of the five fields. The five fields will include the student's ID number, grade, school, school year, and address.

   Divide the address into three sections: (1) name, (2) street address, and (3) city (no state need be included). With the city, allot five spaces for the zip code. Each of these three sections must begin in a predetermined column.

   Use column 80 for a master card punch (a 12-row punch will be used to permit the sorter to separate all master cards from grade cards after the reports have been mailed).
   Allocate columns 75–79 for zip-code numbers in the address.

EDP 4

ELECTRONIC DATA PROCESSING

INTRODUCTION

The definition of EDP (p. 6) merely modified the definition of IDP (Integrated Data Processing) by including an electronic computer as one component of a system which uses a common-language media. We have previously noted that many automated systems do not have large volumes of data to handle and thus may accomplish a stated objective with less sophisticated devices, such as cards, punched tickets, punched tape, or photographic equipment. When a system is to process large volumes of data at very high rates of speed and with a high degree of accuracy, the electronic computer is brought on the scene. The computer can provide management with more information, faster, and at lower cost per unit of information.

The electronic computer was originally developed during World War II to solve scientific and engineering problems. Only within the last decade has the computer found its place in business. Although the early installation of computer systems occurred in only very large business structures, recent developments in computer production have reduced the size and the price of computers so that a great many more businesses can use small- and medium-sized computers. Most businessmen readily acknowledge that the computer has all but "snowed" them under in paper because of the tremendous volume of information it produces; but although the paper volume has increased substantially, the information made

Courtesy of the IBM Corporation.

available is more complete and accurate and permits greater efficiency in business operations.

The following pages deal with the basic operations of computers and how computers may be applied to processing business data.

PROGRAMMING CONCEPT

One of the most perplexing ideas about computers is "How does it know what to do?" "Where does it get its ideas and material to perform the specific jobs that it does?" Once we understand how data is handled, the entire concept of a computer will become clearer.

We are really asking, "How does it keep its data and instructions so it can use what it wants?" Most of us have seen the post office boxes used to hold mail for the persons who rent these boxes. So that the mail will be correctly placed in individual boxes, each box is assigned a different number, an address within the post office used to store only the mail of the person who rents the box. Instead of a street address, the person has a post office box address. The important fact is that mail is circulated by assigned *addresses* in terms of box numbers.

A computer resembles a post office because it has storage facilities into which we can insert data and assign that data to an address (a post office box number). When the computer needs data, it goes to the specific address (box number), reads the data contained within the address (post office box), interprets the data read (finds out what the letter says), and does what the data says to do (answer, discard, or do whatever is desired as a result of reading the letter).

Storage facilities

1	2	3	4
5	6	7	8
9	10	11	12
13	14	15	16

Imagine, then, that we have a computer "post office" with 16 storage boxes (like the post office storage boxes). Each box has an address (a number assigned to it to identify the location, such as the numbers assigned to post office boxes). Because we shall be putting data (letters) into the various boxes until the computer (the post office box rentee) comes to get the data, we call these 16 boxes our *storage* facility.

Assume now that certain data has been put into some of the storage boxes; then the data in the storage boxes would resemble letters or mail put into 16 mail boxes. The accompanying diagram illustrates our 16-box computer and shows what data or "message" has been placed in the various boxes.

Notice, and this is very important, that we now have two kinds of data or "messages" placed in the storage boxes—instructions and figures. The instructions tell us (1) where to go (the address) to get the necessary data (figures) to work with; (2) what to do with

Contents contained in storage addresses

1 Instruction 1	2 Instruction 2	3 Instruction 3	4 Instruction 4
Write down figure contained in Box 16 Go to Box 2	Multiply what you wrote down by figure contained in Box 12 Go to Box 3	Add to what you now have the figure contained in Box 13 Go to Box 4	Multiply what you have by the figure contained in Box 16 Go to Box 5
5 Instruction 5	6 Instruction 6	7 Instruction 7	8
Add to what you now have the figure contained in Box 14 Go to Box 6	Record your answer	Assign a different numeric value in Box 16 Go to Box 1	
9	10	11	12 Figure Value of <u>2</u>
13 Figure Value of <u>4</u>	14 Figure Value of <u>5</u>	15	16 Figure Value of <u>X</u>

the data (add, multiply, record, etc.); (3) where to go (the address) to find the next instruction after the present one is completed.

In some of the storage addresses in our example, certain data in terms of a message or a figure has been placed in the addresses. Seven of the addresses have instructions in them, and four of the addresses have numeric values in them. (Four addresses are not needed for the first illustration of our imaginary computer.)

Using the contents of the storage addresses in the illustration on page 126, let's start with Instruction 1 and go through the addresses (boxes) doing what each instruction tells us to do.

Address (Box Number)	Instruction	Result
1	Write down the figure contained in Box 16; then go to Box 2 for the next instruction.	x
2	Multiply what you have written down (x) by the value contained in Box 12 (value of 2); then go to Box 3 for the next instruction.	$2(x)$ or $2x$
3	Add to what you now have computed $(2x)$ the value contained in Box 13 (value of 4); then go to Box 4 for the next instruction.	$(2x) + 4$ or $2x + 4$
4	Multiply what has been computed up to this point $(2x + 4)$ by the value contained in Box 16 (x); then go to Box 5 for the next instruction.	$(2x + 4)x$ or $2x^2 + 4x$
5	Add to what has been computed $(2x^2 + 4x)$ the value contained in Box 14 (5); then go to Box 6 for the next instruction.	$(2x^2 + 4x) + 5$ or $2x^2 + 4x + 5$
6	Record the answer you have computed.	$2x^2 + 4x + 5$

By following the directions contained within the various addresses in our small computer, we have arrived at the answer of

$2x^2 + 4x + 5$. Actually, we have merely formulated an equation section that contained a variable called x. Now let's see how this part of an equation contained within the storage addresses would function if a number replaced the x variable; let's assume the number to be stored in Address 16 is "3" rather than the x variable. Our computation would be as follows:

Address (Box Number)	Instruction	Result
1	Write down the figure contained in Box 16 (3); then go to Box 2 for next instruction.	3
2	Multiply what you have written down (3) by the value contained in Box 12 (value of 2); then go to Box 3 for next instruction.	(3)2 or 6
3	Add to what you have computed (6) the value contained in Box 13 (value of 4); then go to Box 4 for next instruction.	(6) + 4 or 10
4	Multiply what has been computed to this point (10) by the value contained in Box 16 (value of 3); then go to Box 5 for next instruction.	(10)3 or 30
5	Add to what has been computed (30) the value contained in Box 14 (value of 5); then go to Box 6 for next instruction.	(30) + 5 or 35
6	Record the answer you have computed.	35

After recording the answer, as instructed in Box 6, we might insert still a different number in Box 16, as instructed in Box 7 (p. 126). The new number would be placed in Box 16; then we would return to Box 1 to begin the entire series over again. Let us assume the number "3" that was in Box 16 has been removed and the number "7" inserted. Following the same sequence of operations as we did before for number "3" we would have the following computations:

formula: $2x^2 + 4x + 5 =$ answer

Box 16 Value 3		Box 16 Value 7
3	*Instruction 1* Record value in Box 16	7
6	*Instruction 2* Multiply by value in Box 12 (2)	14
10	*Instruction 3* Add value in Box 13 (4)	18
30	*Instruction 4* Multiply by value in Box 16	126
35	*Instruction 5* Add value in Box 14 (5)	131
35	*Instruction 6* Record answer	131

By using the formula stored in the boxes, we can calculate any value we assign to the x stored in Box 16. Once we have our instructions, it is simple to calculate the various answers resulting from the values we place in Box 16.

Notice in the preceding illustrations that two different types of data were placed in the boxes: (1) constant data, such as instructions that remained the same regardless of what figures were used in addresses 12 through 16; (2) variable data, such as the figures x, 3, and 7 that were changed in Address 16. Another term for the constants which served as instructions for the operations is a *stored program*. The program must be stored in the machine's storage facilities before any data can be properly processed. The program represents a detailed solution to a problem, and the instructions must be followed as directed.

To be sure that we understand the principles involved in programming, let's examine an additional problem. The 16 storage addresses contain the following instructions and data (10 instructions, 4 data, and 2 blanks).

To apply the list of constant instructions (Addresses 1–10) and variable data (Addresses 12–15) given on the following pages, assume that the 16 addresses contain the following information that permits us to compute the weekly pay for one of our employees:

Address 12: (data) Value of A
Total hours worked (we must pay time-and-a-half for all hours over 40)

Address 13: (data) Value of B
Employee's wage rate (per hour)

Address 14: (data) Value of C
Federal income tax withheld (as figured from his declared dependents)

Address 15: (data) Value of D
Total of other deductions (medical insurance, union dues, etc.)

1) Instruction 1	2) Instruction 2	3) Instruction 3	4) Instruction 4
Subtract 40 from figure in Address 12 -- if answer is − or 0, go to Address 2; if answer is +, go to Address 3	Multiply figure in Address 12 by figure in Address 13	Multiply figure in Address 13 by 40; place answer in Address 16	Subtract 40 from figure in Address 12 and multiply answer by 1½
Go to Address 3	Go to Address 7	Go to Address 4	Go to Address 5
5) Instruction 5	6) Instruction 6	7) Instruction 7	8) Instruction 8
Multiply answer from Instruction 4 by figure in Address 13	Add answer from Instruction 5 to figure in Address 16	Subtract figure in Address 14	Subtract figure in Address 15
Go to Address 6	Go to Address 7	Go to Address 8	Go to Address 9
9) Instruction 9	10) Instruction 10	11)	12) Data
Record answer	Store new data in Adresses 12, 13, 14, and 15	Blank	Value of A Total hours worked
Go to Address 10	Go to Address 1		
13) Data	14) Data	15) Data	16)
Value of B Employee's wage rate	Value of C Federal income tax withheld	Value of D Total other deductions	Blank

Now assume that our first employee has the following data inserted into Addresses 12–15:

Address 12: *36* (hours worked during week)

Address 13: *$4.00* (hourly wage rate)

Address 14: *$14.00* (Federal income tax withheld)

Address 15: *$7.50* (total other deductions)

We now have the necessary instructions (stored program) and employee data to compute our first employee's payroll.

Address 1 (Instruction 1) contains the instruction for us to subtract the value of 40 from the value contained in Address 12, 36 (hours worked during the week). This particular instruction deals with an operation in programming known as *branching*; that is, we may be directed to follow the next instruction in line or to skip farther down the line to some other instruction (for further discussion on branching see p. 137). This examination of a condition for a sign (+, −, or 0) permits us to deviate from the main flow of instructions on the basis of a comparison of values—a comparison resulting in a plus value, a minus value, or an equal value. In the case of our first employee, we are told to compare 36 to 40, to subtract 40 from 36. If 36 − 40 gives us a minus (−) figure or an equal value (0), our instructions tell us to go to Address 2 (Instruction 2) for the next operation; if the employee would have had more than 40 hours, we would have had a positive value after the subtraction and thus been directed to Address 3 (Instruction 3).

Address 2 (Instruction 2) tells us to multiply the figure in Address 12, 36 hours worked, by the figure in Address 13, $4.00, the hourly wage rate. The computer is now performing the multiplication of 36 × $4.00 = $144.00. Notice the instruction then tells us to skip several instructions and go to Address 7.

Address 7 (Instruction 7) tells us to subtract the value contained in Address 14, $14.00 withheld for Federal income taxes; and then go to Address 8 for the next instruction. We now have $144.00 − $14.00, or $130.00, a result to carry to the next instruction, Address 8.

Address 8 (Instruction 8) directs us to Address 15 where we are to find the total of our employee's other deductions and subtract this amount. The total for other deductions stored in Address 15 for our first employee is $7.50; when this amount is subtracted from the $130.00 remaining from the previous instruction, we have a new total of $130.00 — $7.50, or $122.50. We are to go to Address 9 for our next instruction.

Address 9 (Instruction 9) informs us that the employee's weekly pay has been computed. We are to record this amount, $122.50, and then go to Address 10.

Address 10 (Instruction 10) directs us to replace the data we had for our first employee in Addresses 12–15 and to place new data for our next employee in these addresses. After the new data has been stored in the four addresses, we are told to go back to Address 1, which is the start of the computation of our new employee's pay.

In summary, we have performed the following operations according to the instructions stored in the addresses used:

Instruction Number	Operation	Result
1	Determine which of two sequences to follow.	Follow minus or zero route
2	Multiply hours worked by the hourly wage rate.	36 hours worked × $4.00 hourly rate ——— $144.00
7	Subtract Federal income tax withheld.	$144.00 — 14.00 tax withheld ——— $130.00
8	Subtract other deductions.	$130.00 — 7.50 other deductions ——— $122.50
9	Record answer.	$122.50 recorded
10	Insert data for next employee.	—

Note that in the instructions in Addresses 1–10, the contents of the addresses remain the same and are called *constants*; only the "variable" data, data in Addresses 12–15, is changed for each employee.

Now assume that employee 2 has the following data:

Address 12: *44*   (hours worked during week)

Address 13: $5.00   (hourly wage rate)

Address 14: $26.00   (Federal income tax withheld)

Address 15: $9.50   (total other deductions)

Let's go through the program once again. This time we will use the foregoing data for employee 2.

> *Address 1* (Instruction 1) orders us to subtract the value of 40 from employee 2's total hours worked, 44 hours. After performing the subtraction of $44 - 40 = 4$ we note we have a positive $(+4)$ rather than a negative answer. Because of the positive answer, we are instructed to go to Address 3 for our next instruction. (In processing employee 1, we went to Address 2 because we had a negative answer.) This branching operation performed in Address 1 (Instruction 1) was necessary because two possible situations existed: either an employee works 40 hours or less and thus no extra computatation is required to determine the number of overtime hours worked, such as the situation for employee 1; or an employee works more than 40 hours a week and thus time-and-a-half must be paid to him for those hours in excess of the regular 40-hour work week, such as the situation for employee 2. To arrive at the gross pay for employee 2 (total pay due the employee before any deductions are subtracted), we must (1) multiply the hours on the regular work week (40 hours) by his hourly work rate ($5.00); (2) multiply the hours in excess of 40 (the overtime hours of 4) by 1½ times to provide for the time-and-a-half overtime ($4 \times 1½ = 6$ overtime hours); (3) multiply the overtime hours (6) by the hourly wage rate ($5.00); (4) add the regular wage and the overtime wage for the total pay due. These calculations are performed in the instructions located in Addresses 3, 4, 5, and 6. These four addresses were skipped in com-

puting the pay for employee 1 because no overtime pay was involved.

Address 3 (Instruction 3) tells us to multiply the number of hours of the regular work week (40 hours) by the hourly wage rate assigned to Address 13 and then place this answer in Address 16 for temporary storage. Address 16 does not contain any constant instruction or any data taken from employee 2. This figure that was calculated, the 40 × $5.00 = $200.00 for the regular work week, must be temporarily stored so that no figures are carried forward within the computer's calculating section when it starts to compute the overtime hours for employee 2. After determining the overtime pay, we go back to Address 16, take out the regular pay ($200.00) that we temporarily stored, and add regular pay to the overtime pay in order to arrive at the total pay (gross pay) due employee 2.

Address 4 (Instruction 4) directs us to subtract 40 (total regular hours) from 44 (total hours worked as stored in Address 12). We now have the number of overtime hours he has worked, 44 — 40 = 4 overtime hours. Instruction 4 also tells us to multiply the number of overtime hours we calculated (4 hours) by 1½ times to arrive at the figure to be used to evaluate his overtime pay, 4 × 1½ = 6 overtime hours. Our instructions now tell us to go to Address 5.

Address 5 (Instruction 5) tells us to multiply the number of hours he is credited for his overtime (6 hours) by the hourly wage rate stored in Address 13 ($5.00 per hour); 6 × $5.00 = $30.00, or the amount earned by working the extra hours beyond the 40-hour work week. We are then to go to Instruction 6.

Address 6 (Instruction 6) tells us to add the overtime pay ($30.00) just computed to the regular pay ($200.00) computed in Instruction 3 and then stored in Address 16. So, we shall go to Address 16, bring back the $200.00 regular pay, and add the $30.00 overtime pay to it in order to get a total pay (gross) of $230.00. Then we are to go to Address 7.

Address 7 (Instruction 7) is the start of the deductions to be taken from an employee's total or gross pay. Remember that, for employee 1 (p. 131), we went directly from Address 2 to Address 7 because we had no overtime pay to calculate. Address 7 will be included in the computation of the pay for all our employees. This instruction tells us to subtract the value in Address 14 ($26.00 for Federal income tax withheld) from the $230.00 earned by employee 2—$230.00 — $26.00 = $204.00 due our employee. Go to Address 8.

Address 8 (Instruction 8) directs us to subtract the remaining deductions as stored in Address 15 ($9.50) which leave $204.00 — $9.50 = $194.50 that will be paid to employee 2. We are to go to Address 9 for the next instruction.

Address 9 (Instruction 9) tells us to record the amount of net pay we are to give employee 2 ($194.50); and then to go to Address 10 for the next instruction.

Address 10 (Instruction 10) directs us to replace the data pertaining to employee 2 just used in Addresses 12–15 with the payroll data pertaining to the next employee, employee 3. After the new data has been placed in these four addresses, we are told to go back to Address 1 and begin the process of determining the net pay for employee 3.

For employee 2, we have performed the following operations previously described:

Instruction Number	Operation	Result
1	Determine which of two sequences to follow.	Follow plus route
3	Multiply weekly wage rate by 40 to get regular pay.	$5.00 wage rate × 40 regular hours $200.00 regular pay
4	Subtract 40 from total hours worked to get overtime hours and multiply by 1½.	44 total hours — 40 regular hours 4 overtime hours × 1½ 6 hours

5	Multiply hours by hourly wage rate.	6 hours $\times$ \$5.00 wage rate $\overline{\text{\$30.00}}$ overtime pay
6	Add regular pay to overtime pay to get gross pay.	\$30.00 overtime pay 200.00 regular pay $\overline{\text{\$230.00}}$ gross pay
7	Substract Federal income tax withheld.	\$230.00 gross pay — 26.00 tax withheld $\overline{\text{\$204.00}}$
8	Subtract other deductions.	\$204.00 — 9.50 other deductions recorded $\overline{\text{\$194.50}}$
9	Record answer.	\$194.50
10	Store new data for next employee and return to beginning instructions.	

Notice that we were directed to return to the beginning instructions to continue processing the payroll for each of our employees. After we determined the net pay for employee 1, we inserted the data for employee 2 and then determined his net pay; after we determined the net pay for employee 2, we were told to insert the data for employee 3 and return to the beginning instructions again. The computer's ability to return to the beginning of a sequence and repeat the instructions is called *looping*. Looping is one of the most important functions of the computer and will be discussed several times in remaining sections.

Two primary advantages of the use of the computer are (1) its capacity to select a specific operational sequence to follow (branching), (2) its ability to complete these selected sequences many, many times (looping) at extremely rapid speeds. We may be stretching the point a bit when we say that branching operations direct the course of action on the basis of a decision reached by the computer. Actually, the computer is merely comparing two values and then following the course predetermined in the instructions we have given it.

For example, we could have stopped the processing of payroll

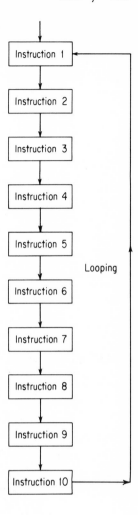

Looping

checks in the preceding payroll illustration by using a "branch" operation—a comparison of two numbers. Remember, the direction of a sequence of operations following a branch operation can be determined on the basis of three possible conditions: (1) a + (positive) answer; (2) a — (negative) answer; (3) a 0 (zero or equal) answer. Assume, then, that we had 450 employees working for us. If we set up a branching operation on the basis of a comparison of the $450 - x$ (let x be the number of employees processed), as soon as the comparison produces a 0 (zero) answer $(450 - 450 = 0)$, we shall have the computer stop operations because we shall have processed all 450 of our employees. Until we arrive at a 0 (zero) answer, we shall have the computer return to the beginning and repeat the payroll process once again in a looping process, as we did after we found the pay due employees 1 and 2 in the preceding payroll illustration. Not until 450 loops have been completed will the computer stop processing.

Branch Number	Employee Number			Result
450	—	1	= 449	Positive value; return to process next employee.
450	—	2	= 448	Positive value; return to process next employee.
450	—	3	= 447	Positive value; return to process next employee.
	. . .			(Employee numbers continue to increase by 1.)
450	—	448	= 2	Positive value; return to process next employee.
450	—	449	= 1	Positive value; return to process next employee.
450	—	450	= 0	Zero value; last employee processed; stop operations.

After each employee's pay has been determined in the preceding illustration, a value of 1 is added to the number of employees who have been processed. After the first employee's record has been processed (assuming he has been assigned the value of 1) an operation, such as $x + 1$, will serve as a counter and will eventually tell us when $x + 1 + 1$ . . . will accumulate to a value of 450, the value necessary to order a branching operation to a "stop processing" command.

Routine business data that merely requires a repetition of the processing instructions over and over again is very common; and here the important procedure of looping becomes so valuable. In order to return to the beginning again and repeat the instructions, it is usually necessary that the computer analyze the values resulting from a branching operation, such as the one just presented. Therefore, looping is a result of a branch operation; but a given branch operation need not always result in a looping operation. In the preceding example, a branch to a looping operation will result until the value accumulates to 450; when, however, 450 is subtracted and the answer is zero, the branch will be to a stop operation rather than to a looping operation.

As previously mentioned, a branch operation could direct the following sequences to one of three different processing routines: a positive ($+$) routine, a negative ($-$) routine, or a zero (0) routine. For example, assume that you have three different types or classifications of workers in your business. One is the salesman paid on the basis of how much merchandise he sells. This worker gets a

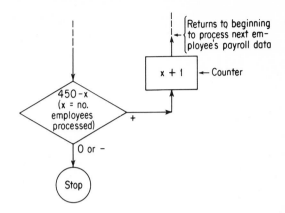

commission on his total sales; therefore, you must compute his weekly pay by taking a percentage of the total sales made by each salesman included in your payroll. A second classification is the hourly worker paid on the basis of how many hours per week he works multiplied by the hourly wage rate he receives—the method used to compute the pay in the previous payroll example. The third group of workers is the executive who receives an annual salary; thus a set portion is paid each week without regard to sales made or hours worked.

So you have three different methods for paying your employees. Each method requires a distinctly different procedure to be followed for computing a worker's pay. You must have three different procedures to follow in your payroll program. Perhaps you might assign each of your employees an employee number corresponding to the three different groups: salesmen, regular workers, and executives. It is easier to process numbers than alphabetic titles or names. Salesmen might have any number in a 1000 series: 1001, 1002, 1003, etc. Regular employees, clerks, production line workers etc., might start with a 200 series: 2001, 2002, 2003, etc. Executives might be assigned numbers in the 3000 series: 3001, 3002, 3003, etc.

Classification Number	Worker Classification	
1,000	Salesmen	Pay based on commission (% of total sales)
2,000	Regular employees	Pay based on hourly wage rate
3,000	Executives	Pay based on annual salary (no variation in pay from payroll to payroll)

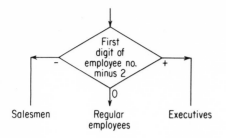

When payroll data is given to the computer to be processed, the employee number in the data will be used to tell the computer which of the three sequences the computer is to follow to process the pay. How? By the "branching" procedure described earlier. If you use only the "thousand's" digit (the fourth digit from the right) while disregarding the other three digits, and if you subtract a value of 2 from that "thousand's" digit, you will have three possible sequences to follow:

Employee Number	Minus a Value of 2		Result
1000	1 — 2	=	Negative value
2000	2 — 2	=	Zero value
3000	3 — 2	=	Positive value
(disregard these digits)			

For example, if an employee's number of 1649 is given to the computer, the computer will read only the thousand's digit (the 1), subtract a value of 2 from the 1, obtain a negative answer, and then direct the payroll processing to the program designed to compute the salesman's pay. If an employee's number is 2009, the computer will read the 2, subtract a value of 2, obtain a zero answer, and follow the program for the regular employees. If the number should happen to be 3071, the computer will read the 3, subtract 2, and follow the "positive" sequence for executives.

As just illustrated, branching operations do not necessarily imply that a looping procedure must follow in sequence; looping may or may not follow a branching operation. On the other hand, if we do have a looping procedure, we must have had a branch operation. The computer must have made its "decision" whether to repeat (perform a loop) or to continue with new instructions that have not been completed.

Most data processing in business contains some looping procedures. Basically, the instructions within the loops always remain the same for all subsequent passes. The data used within the loops, however, will change. Each time a new group of input data is given to the computer to be processed, the arithmetic results will be different unless the input data is exactly the same as the data previously processed. By using the counting device illustrated (p. 138), the computer can use different numbers in each pass through the loop; the instructions may remain the same, such as $x + 1$, but the results of the computations will change because different data was given for the computations. When we have large amounts of repetitive data, as in payroll operations, application of the looping principle is the very foundation of the data processing procedure.

DIAGRAMMING CONCEPT

If you were instructed to buy one typewriter ribbon that sold for $24 a dozen and were given a $5 bill to make the purchase, you would have no problem in returning with the typewriter ribbon and with $3 in change—you could reason that $24 ÷ 12 = $2 per ribbon and $5 − $2 = $3 change. You are much smarter than the most powerful computer in existence. Because of your past experiences, you can perform without detailed and literal instructions. You can make your own decisions based on judgment involving many, many factors. But a computer is completely helpless unless it can "parrot" what it has previously heard. Unless it receives a complete, detailed list of instructions that tell it what to do for each and every circumstance that may arise, this mechanical "brain" is unable to proceed. It can do only what it has been told to do, not what the operator would like it to do.

The problem, then, is preparing a list of instructions to be performed in a designated sequence, which provide for all possible situations that may arise during the processing operations. Such an orderly list of inclusive instructions can be prepared only if the programmer has a thorough comprehension of the problem. Because most persons are unable to visualize mentally all the possible details of a specific problem, programmers use graphic aids and insert short descriptions to designate the sequences to be followed, the conditions to be met, the operations to be performed, and other information that will help later in compiling a complete set of detailed instructions needed for a computer to solve a given problem. Nett and Hetzler note that writing a program

... is like running a train from coast to coast, making sure that each switch is set correctly following its last use, being prepared to change the route at every switch should alternate conditions which must be kept account of occur, maintaining a precise knowledge of coincidence of timing at all points, making emergency preparations for every external intervention that could reasonably be anticipated, and doing all of this projectedly—that is before the trip is started—since we cannot be allowed to travel with it.*

To help programmers keep track of logical operations and sequences in which the operations must flow, programmers present their suggested solutions in schematic or diagrammatic forms called *block diagrams*. Unfortunately, the shapes of blocks used in the diagrams to represent different processing operations have not been standardized; some of the more commonly accepted shapes, and those used throughout this book, are as follows:

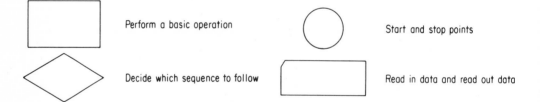

Perform a basic operation

Start and stop points

Decide which sequence to follow

Read in data and read out data

On p. 143 is a block diagram showing a common occurrence in our daily lives. This diagram illustrates the basic operations required for a phonograph to play various sizes of records. This particular phonograph determines where the tone arm is to be placed for playing records by first having the tone arm move from its "rest" position toward the unplayed records stacked on the spindle, touching the stacked records, returning to the "rest" position, dropping one record, moving back to the proper position for playing the dropped record, and releasing the recorded tones. Within this sequence is a *major loop*—the reverting back to the beginning to play another record—and a *minor loop*—a constant looping se-

* Roger Nett and Stanley A. Hetzler, *An Introduction to Electronic Data Processing* (Glencoe, Ill.: The Fress Press, 1959), p. 110.

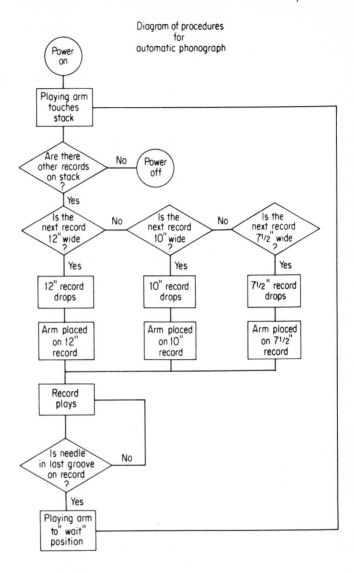

Diagram of procedures
for
automatic phonograph

quence that continues throughout the playing of each record until the needle arrives in the groove that rapidly moves it toward the center of the record to signify the end of the record.

The block diagram which follows represents the payroll problem to be described on pp. 182–193. Note the starting and stopping points and the two branching operations: one continues or stops the processing of net pay of each succeeding employee; the other decides to process either overtime or regular pay.

As may be noted in this diagram, the descriptions within the blocks are not complete in detail. For example, the descriptions in

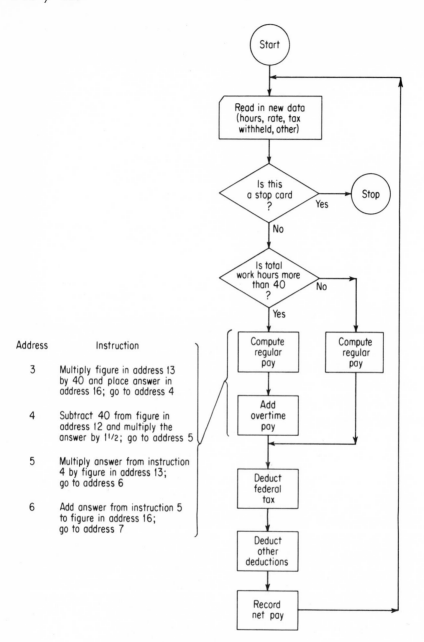

the two blocks "Compute regular pay" and "Add overtime pay" do not contain the detailed instructions shown in the completed program (see p. 130).

Address	Instruction
3	Multiply figure in Address 13 by 40 and place answer in Address 16; go to Address 4.

4   Subtract 40 from figure in Address 12 and multiply the answer by 1½; go to Address 5.

5   Multiply answer from Instruction 4 by figure in Address 13; go to Address 6.

6   Add answer from Instruction 5 to figure in Address 16; go to Address 7.

Block diagrams may be drawn to show any desired degree of detail. In long, complicated problems, the first block diagram will contain only simple, undetailed blocks. Several succeeding diagrams may be required before sufficient detail is included to permit a programmer to write a set of computer instructions from the final block diagrams. He is assisted if the descriptions in the blocks approximate the type of wording actually used by the programmer when writing the final instructions. Since highly complicated business problems may take a hundred or more pages of detailed instructions before the actual processing can begin, detailed block diagrams illustrating the flow of sequences to be followed are extremely important in solving business problems. The payroll problem previously presented is a highly simplified illustration used only to present some programming and diagramming principles. An actual payroll problem would be much longer and much more complicated. For example, any number of the 67 deductions listed at the right may be withheld from the net pay of an employee of the state of California, and each of the 67 possibilities must be provided for in the payroll program.

MISCELLANEOUS DEDUCTIONS

CODE	EXPLANATION
02	SERS NORMAL CONTRIBUTION ADJUSTMENT (NO SERVICE)
03	SERS ARREARS NORMAL CONTRIBUTIONS (SERVICE)
04	SERS OTHER MISCELLANEOUS CONTRIBUTIONS
08	SERS ADDITIONAL CONTRIBUTIONS
10	CWSL/CSEA MAJOR MEDICAL INSURANCE, LIFE INSURANCE
11	MAINTENANCE
12	SEABOARD LIFE INSURANCE CO. OF AMERICA
13	WASHINGTON NAT'L./CALIF.-ASSN. HIGHWAY PATROLMEN – LIFE INSURANCE
15	KAISER FOUNDATION HEALTH PLAN, INC., NORTHERN REGION
16	DUES IN CALIFORNIA STATE EMPLOYEES ASSN.
17	CHARITABLE CONTRIBUTIONS
18	BLUE CROSS PLAN/VARIOUS EMPLOYEE ASSOCIATIONS INSURANCE – MAJOR MEDICAL
20	CPS/CSEA INSURANCE – MAJOR MEDICAL
25	FEDERATED LIFE INSURANCE CO./ACSCP INSURANCE – INCOME PROTECTION, MAJOR MEDICAL
30	TAX SHELTERED ANNUITIES
31	TEACHER'S RETIREMENT ADJUSTMENT
32	JUDGE'S RETIREMENT ADJUSTMENT
33	GOVERNMENT LIFE INSURANCE
35	ACCOUNTS RECEIVABLE
36	U.S. SAVINGS BONDS
37	OLD LINE LIFE INSURANCE CO. OF AMERICA (CCCFT)
38	CONTINENTAL CASUALTY COMPANY (USE 411)
39	JUDGMENT
40	RAILROAD RETIREMENT ADJUSTMENT
42	MUTUAL LIFE INS. CO. OF N.Y./CSEA INSURANCE – INCOME PROTECTION
43	INSURANCE COMPANY OF NORTH AMERICA
44	NEW YORK LIFE INSURANCE COMPANY
45	PACIFIC NATIONAL LIFE ASSURANCE COMPANY
47	CONTINENTAL CASUALTY COMPANY
49	CONTRIBUTIONS TO UNION TRUST FUNDS (CASUAL EMPLOYMENT)
50	PARKING
51	CREDIT UNION
53	CWSL/SERS INSURANCE – MEDICAL AND HOSPITAL CARE
56	KAISER FOUNDATION – NORTHERN CALIF./SERS OR CSEA – MEDICAL AND HOSPITAL CARE
57	KAISER FOUNDATION – SOUTHERN CALIF./SERS OR CSEA – MEDICAL AND HOSPITAL CARE
58	ROSS-LOOS MEDICAL GROUP/SERS OR CSEA – MEDICAL AND HOSPITAL CARE
59	PSA/SERS INSURANCE – MEDICAL AND HOSPITAL CARE
60	BLUE CROSS/BLUE SHIELD/SERS OR CSEA – STANDARD PLAN MEDICAL AND HOSPITAL CARE
62	COUNTY MEDICAL SOCIETIES/SERS – MEDICAL AND HOSPITAL CARE
63	CWSL/SERS SUPPLEMENT TO MEDICARE – MEDICAL AND HOSPITAL CARE
64	BLUE CROSS-BLUE SHIELD/SERS OR CSEA SUPPLEMENT TO MEDICARE – MEDICAL AND HOSPITAL CARE
65	COUNTY MEDICAL SOCIETIES/SERS SUPPLEMENT TO MEDICARE – MEDICAL AND HOSPITAL CARE
66	KAISER FOUNDATION – NO. CALIF./SERS OR CSEA SUPPLEMENT TO MEDICARE – MEDICAL AND HOSPITAL CARE
67	KAISER FOUNDATION – SO. CALIF./SERS OR CSEA SUPPLEMENT TO MEDICARE – MEDICAL AND HOSPITAL CARE
68	ROSS-LOOS/SERS OR CSEA SUPPLEMENT TO MEDICARE – MEDICAL AND HOSPITAL CARE
77	SERS SURVIVORS BENEFITS CONTRIBUTION
79	THE WESTERN AND SOUTHERN LIFE INSURANCE CO.
80	BLUE CROSS/ASSN., CALIFORNIA HIGHWAY PATROLMEN – MEDICAL AND HOSPITAL CARE
81	BLUE CROSS/FISH AND GAME WARDENS' PROTECTIVE ASSN. – MEDICAL AND HOSPITAL CARE
82	FEDERATED LIFE INSURANCE CO./ACSCP INSURANCE – MEDICAL AND HOSPITAL CARE
83	BLUE CROSS/CTA INSURANCE – MEDICAL AND HOSPITAL CARE
84	INTERCOAST LIFE INSURANCE CO.
85	OCCIDENTAL LIFE INSURANCE CO. OF CALIF. – CSEA.
86	OLD LINE LIFE INSURANCE CO. OF AMERICA
87	OCCIDENTAL LIFE INSURANCE CO. OF NORTH CAROLINA (PESA)
88	DUES IN MISCELLANEOUS EMPLOYEE ASSOCIATIONS (OTHER THAN CSEA)
89	OCCIDENTAL LIFE INSURANCE CO. OF CALIF. – CTA
90	NORTH AMERICAN INSURANCE (CSC)
91	CALIFORNIA LIFE INSURANCE COMPANY (PESA)
92	CALIFORNIA LIFE INSURANCE COMPANY (USE NO.411)
93	CERTIFIED LIFE INSURANCE CO. OF CALIFORNIA
94	CALIFORNIA FEDERATION OF TEACHERS INSURANCE TRUST
95	CALIFORNIA STATE INCOME TAX
96	NEW YORK STATE INCOME TAX
97	OLD AGE, SURVIVORS, AND DISABILITY INSURANCE
98	CALIFORNIA UNEMPLOYMENT DISABILITY INSURANCE
99	FEDERAL WITHHOLDING TAX ADJUSTMENT

IBM J80385

CODING CONCEPT

A block diagram is designed to make visible the sequences of the general operations needed to complete a problem and thus to formalize the logic of the program. Once the logic and sequences have been diagrammed graphically to illustrate in detail the general processing steps needed to execute a certain problem, the detailed information within the proper blocks must be converted into instructions written in a language comprehensible to the computer which is to perform the processing operations. This conversion of a block diagram into machine language is called *coding*.

Our previous comparison of a "post office" facility to an electronic computer must end at this point. As the remainder of our discussions of computers makes clear, there are several functions of data processing that are characteristic of computers only. Even within the family of computers, there is considerable variation in operation procedures. We shall devise our own IMaginary COMputer (IMCOM) to illustrate basic operating functions.

Like all computers, IMCOM cannot understand English, but IMCOM does have its own mechanical language, and we must translate English words into IMCOM words if we are to communicate with IMCOM. Again, it is imperative to remember that, like all computers, IMCOM is not capable of "thinking." It has no imagination; it cannot improvise; it can only follow directions and do what it has been told to do. Therefore, we must be certain that we communicate with IMCOM clearly and unambiguously. IMCOM would be completely helpless without our instructions, but with our accurate, detailed instructions, we can expect IMCOM to do what it is directed to do and to do it without error.

Our problem, then, is twofold: (1) We must provide IMCOM with proper instructions in the proper sequences. (2) We must provide IMCOM with the necessary data to be processed. Both instructions and data must be in IMCOM's own language.

Unlike English, which contains words of variable length (from 1 to 29 letters), IMCOM's language is made up of 10-letter words only; and each word has three syllables. Here we must again downgrade IMCOM's intelligence and ability; IMCOM cannot understand letters. All communication with IMCOM must be by numbers; therefore, we must use some type of code to change English "letter" words into IMCOM's "number" words.

The first "syllable," or the first two digits, in a 10-digit word will be a coded number designating some type of operation, such as add, subtract, multiply, or divide. Instead of telling IMCOM to "add," we merely tell it to "10." How does it know that the code 10 means the same thing as "add?" The various code numbers we will use with IMCOM have been mechanically built into IMCOM so that IMCOM can perform the specific operations assigned to it. When we use a desk calculator and add one number to another, we merely depress a key or a bar (possibly with a + marked on it), and the calculator gives us the result of the addition. The "add" key has been built into the calculator so that it always performs an addition operation when depressed by the operator. IMCOM has been similarly built except that there are no "add" keys to depress. A reading of the numbered code of "10" is recognized by IMCOM as an instruction to add, just as the depressing of the "add" key on a desk calculator is recognized by the calculator as an "add" instruction.

Large computers have many "built-in" operations that are assigned code numbers, and the operations are performed when the specific code number is read by the computer. For simplicity, we assume that IMCOM has only thirteen operating codes that can be performed within IMCOM. These thirteen codes are as follows:

Mnemonic Aid	Code Number	Operation
RDC	01	Read a card.
PCH	02	Punch a card.
SHR	03	Shift to the right.
SHL	04	Shift to the left.
RLR	05	Reset and load the register.
STR	06	Store in specified location.
BRP	07	Branch on positive number.
BRN	08	Branch on negative number.
HLT	09	Halt operations.
ADD	10	Add.
SUB	11	Subtract.
MUL	12	Multiply.
DIV	13	Divide.

These thirteen operation codes, then, make up the first two digits of each of IMCOM's 10-digit words.

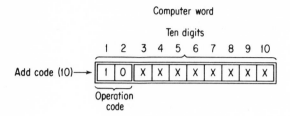

The next four digits in IMCOM's word designate where to go in storage (the address) to find a number or where to put a number. In other words, digits 3, 4, 5, and 6 in the 10-digit word tell the storage address of the data to be used in computation or the address where data already computed is to be stored for later use. This concept of using specific addresses to store data contributes the greatest block to understanding computer operations. The important fact to remember is this:

> The data address (the 3, 4, 5, and 6 digits of a word) tells *only the address* of the data. *It does not tell the value of the number that is stored* in the designated data address.

In our earlier "post office" analogy, the computer's data address in storage is the same as a post office box number; it is not the letter or the message that might be in any specific mail box. Assume that we already have a value of 16 in IMCOM's arithmetic section, and we now want to add a value of 4 to the 16 to get a total of 20. Assume, also, that we know that the address 0707 has a value of 4 stored in it (the 0707 is the post office box number and the value

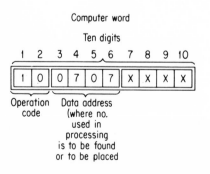

of 4 is the message put into the box). To make the addition possible, we would tell IMCOM to "10" (code for "add") and to use the value stored in Address 0707 (the value of 4).

Recall our previous statement that IMCOM will do only what we tell it to do and will do it in the sequence that we designate. The last four digits in our 10-digit word instructs IMCOM where to go in storage to obtain the next instruction in our designated sequence. Assume that our next instruction is stored in Address 0405. The 7, 8, 9, and 10 digits in the 10-digit word would be 0405, as shown in the accompanying illustration.

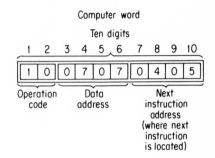

All words used by IMCOM will contain (1) an operation code (first two digits), (2) a data address (next four digits), (3) an instruction address (last four digits). Therefore, each 10-digit word will tell

What operation to perform (add, shift, store, etc.).
Where to find the needed data to be processed, or where to
place the data that has been processed.
What sequence of instructions to follow.

Because the computer words must be in coded form and are thus somewhat difficult for us to read and interpret, program sheets provide additional space for mnemonic aids (abbreviations) and comments. The mnemonic aids and comments are placed on the program sheets, but they are never fed to IMCOM because IMCOM can receive only numbers; the aids and comments are used to help people understand the written program. Each coded operation (see p. 152) also has three letters that indicate what the specific numeric code stands for; for example, code 11 for subtraction carries the mnemonic aid SUB, and this aid would appear on the program sheet next to the numeric code. At the end of each

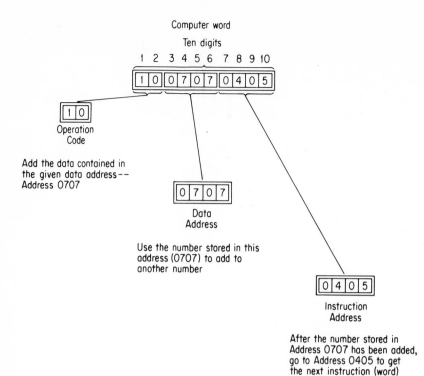

Computer word

Ten digits

1 2 3 4 5 6 7 8 9 10

| 1 | 0 | 0 | 7 | 0 | 7 | 0 | 4 | 0 | 5 |

| 1 | 0 |

Operation
Code

Add the data contained in
the given data address――
Address 0707

| 0 | 7 | 0 | 7 |

Data
Address

Use the number stored in this
address (0707) to add to
another number

| 0 | 4 | 0 | 5 |

Instruction
Address

After the number stored in
Address 0707 has been added,
go to Address 0405 to get
the next instruction (word)
that is to be executed

line on the program sheet additional space is provided under "Remarks" for inserting explanations that the programmer believes would be helpful to anyone who has reason to check the program for errors or to alter the program. The more familiar with a computer's code the programmer and his associates become, the fewer comments need to be inserted.

After we have analyzed each block in our block diagram, written the proper instructions for the desired sequences, translated each instruction from English into computer words, and placed the coded instructions in the computer's storage, we have what is called a *stored program.* This is a self-contained list of instructions designating the procedures necessary to process the variable data that will then be supplied to the computer. When all these steps have been combined into an unvarying list of operations, a stored program, the computer can doggedly follow the chain of detailed instructions at speeds calculated in millionths of seconds.

INPUT

But how do the written program and the data to be processed get into the proper storage addresses within the computer? Almost all the input (data and instructions) used in any data processing system of which a computer is a part requires some human manipulation of a keyboard to get the data into a workable form. There are some exceptions; for example, magnetic ink and optical scanning devices eliminate the preparation of cards, tapes, or other input media. The data is taken from the source documents and fed directly to the computer in a language the computer can understand. But most of our current systems require that some clerical operations be performed before the data can be turned over to the computer for processing.

We have previously noted that IMCOM must be fed two different types of information: (1) the set of instructions that tells IMCOM how to compute the payroll amounts; (2) the payroll data from each employee to be processed. Our instruction program will be entered into IMCOM's storage unit by punched cards, just as the employee data is. We shall restrict IMCOM's capabilities to accepting punched cards only; in actual business situations, data is often entered by punched cards, punched tapes, punched tags or tickets, magnetic tapes, or any other media acceptable to the specific computer being used.

Let us refer to the payroll problem diagrammed earlier (p. 144). We shall not concern ourselves at this point with the details of writing and coding the final program. But from the coded program and punched cards, we can note the following facts:

1. The punched cards contain figures only. The mnemonic aids and the instruction comments shown in the "OPERATION ABBRV" and "REMARKS" columns on the coding sheet are not punched into the cards.

2. The punched cards contain the identical figures listed in the "OPERATION CODE," "ADDRESS DATA," and "ADDRESS INSTR" columns of the coding sheet; the sequence of digits in each word and the sequence of each 10-digit word are exactly the same on the cards as written in the instructions.

3. Each 10-digit coded instruction on the program sheet is punched into the first ten columns of the punched cards, and none of the punched instruction cards contain punches in any columns past Column 10.

Each punched card, then, carries one instruction that will be read

PROBLEM: PAYROLL FOR IMCOM				WRITTEN BY: Langenbach		

INSTR NO.	LOCATION OF INSTR	OPERATION		ADDRESS		REMARKS
		ABBRV	CODE	DATA	INSTR	
1	0400	RDC	01	0900	0401	Read constants into addresses 0900-0907
2	0401	RDC	01	0700	0402	Read Employee data into addresses 0700-0707
3	0402	RLR	05	0700	0403	Reset register to 0; load in Empl. no. from 0700
4	0403	SUB	11	0900	0404	Subtract no. in 0900 (10000) from Empl. no.
5	0404	BRP	07	0423	0405	If answer is +, go to 0423; if − or 0, go to 0405
6	0405	ADD	10	0900	0406	Add back 0900 (10.000) to restore Empl. no.
7	0406	STR	06	1200	0407	Store Empl. no. in address 1200
8	0407	RLR	05	0701	0408	Reset register to 0, load in hrs. worked (0701)
9	0408	SUB	11	0901	0409	Subtract 0901 (40) from hrs. worked
10	0409	BRP	07	0412	0410	If answer is + (more than 40 hrs.) go to 0412; if answer is − or 0 (less or equal to 40 hrs.) go to 0410
11	0410	ADD	10	0901	0411	Add back 0901 (40) to restore hrs. worked
12	0411	MUL	12	0702	0419	Multiply total hours by hourly rate (0702)
13	0412	MUL	12	0902	0413	Multiply overtime hrs. by 1½ (0902)
14	0413	MUL	12	0702	0414	Multiply total overtime hrs. by hourly wage rate
15	0414	SHR	03	0001	0415	Shift answer 1 place to right to compensate for fraction in Instruction 0412
16	0415	STR	06	1201	0416	Store overtime pay in 1201
17	0416	RLR	05	0901	0417	Reset register to 0; load regular hrs. of 40 (0901)
18	0417	MUL	12	0702	0418	Multiply regular hrs. (40) by hourly rate (0702)
19	0418	ADD	10	1201	0419	Add overtime to regular pay to get gross pay
20	0419	SUB	11	0703	0420	Subtract Federal income tax withheld
21	0420	SUB	11	0704	0421	Subtract total other deductions
22	0421	STR	06	1201	0422	Store net pay in Address 1201
23	0422	PCH	02	1200	0401	Punch a card with stored Empl. no. (1200) and net pay (1201); return to address 0401
24	0423	HLT	09	0000	0000	Halt operations

```
0900000000      Last card for
0212000401      last instruction
0612010422
1107040421
1107030420
1012010419
1207020418
0509010417
0612010416
0300010415
1207020414
1209020413
1207020412
1009010411
0704120410
1109010409
0507010408
0612000407
1009000406
0704230405
1109000404
0507000403      First card for
0107000402      first instruction
0109000401
```

CODE, DATA, INSTR sequence on program sheet is same sequence as punched into instruction cards into the storage unit of IMCOM. After all twenty-four coded punched cards are read into the storage addresses, IMCOM has a stored program that it can use to process the employee data cards that may now be read and processed one at a time. For example, when IMCOM begins processing the payroll data, it will come to the second instruction in the program (Instruction 0401) which tells IMCOM to "01" or "Read a card." At this command, the data on one employee punched card is read into the storage unit, and the remainder of the instructions for determining an employee's pay are executed by using the payroll data taken from one employee data card. Not until IMCOM has given us the final net pay figure for the specific employee as computed from the data taken from his data card will the computer go back to the beginning of the program and ask for data pertaining to the next employee.

But, you might question, how do we get the original list of instructions into IMCOM? If it has no instructions in storage addresses in the first place, how can IMCOM ask us to feed it the necessary instructions that it is to perform when it processes our payroll? The method of entering the original list of instructions into a computer's storage unit varies with different makes of computers. Many computers know when instructions are going to be given to them because human operators press certain buttons or keys on the computer console control panel; the buttons signify that the following input cards are instruction cards (not data cards) and the computer is to handle the instructions accordingly. We shall assume that IMCOM, like many other computers, gets its command to accept instructions from specially punched cards. One of these special cards is placed at the beginning of the instruction deck and tells IMCOM, "The following cards are instruction cards; store the coded directions in instruction addresses." Another specially punched card will be placed at the end of the instruction deck; this special "end card" tells IMCOM, "All instructions have been placed in storage; begin processing data by executing Instruction 1 at Address 0400." At this command, IMCOM will go back to the first instruction address (Address 0400) and execute the operation described in the instruction contained in Address 0400 as shown in the program illustrated (p. 152). This first instruction tells IMCOM that the first operation it is to perform is to read a card, store the data of that card in addresses beginning with 0900, and then proceed to the next instruction, Instruction 2, located at Address 0401.

We should consider one other step at this time. Most programmers prefer to begin their own processing of data with a computer that has been completely cleared of all data within its units; all addresses have been set to "zero" or "cleaned" of any data or instructions that may have been stored during the processing of some other program. This process of erasing all previous instructions and data from storage addresses is called *housekeeping*. A computer receives this housekeeping command by reading in a special "clear" card that precedes all other cards, even the instruction notification card mentioned in the foregoing paragraph.

Our sequence of cards that will serve as input to IMCOM will be as follows:

1. Clear card — A housekeeping card to erase all figures that may be in storage addresses as a result of any preceding processing operation.

2. Call card for instructions — An information card indicating that the following cards are to be instruction cards and their contents are to be placed in storage addresses assigned for instructions only.

3. Instruction cards — A deck of cards containing coded instructions to be used to process forthcoming data cards.

4. End card for instructions — An information card indicating that the instructions are now complete and that IMCOM is to go back to the first instruction and begin processing data cards.

5. Data cards — A deck of cards containing specific data on each employee.

Like the instruction cards that had to be punched according to a predetermined format (punching permitted in the first 10 columns only for instructions), the data cards must also be punched according to a specific layout. Although each data card could contain 8 words of data for IMCOM (80 columns per card divided by 10 columns required for each word equals 8 words), our requirements for each employee card in our payroll problem will be only 5 words per card, as will be evident. The allocation of columns in this IMCOM payroll problem remains the same as the allocation used during the discussion of punched cards (see also p. 65).

Word 1 (Columns 1–10)   Employee number

Word 2 (Columns 11–20)   Total hours worked

Word 3 (Columns 21–30)   Hourly wage rate

Word 4 (Columns 31–40)   Federal income tax witheld

Word 5 (Columns 41–50)   Other deductions

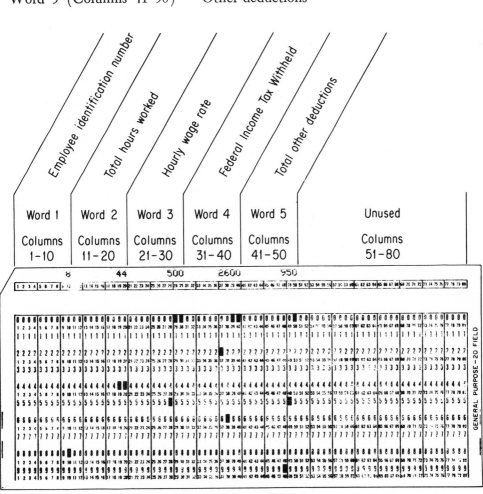

Each of the foregoing specific categories listed must be punched within the card columns assigned to it or IMCOM cannot process the data accurately. We have accepted this sequence of data for this particular problem; if we make any changes in the sequence of the categories or length of words, IMCOM will not be able to recognize these exceptions and will thus process the data incorrectly. An example of the predetermined arrangement or format of data cards is on p. 155. Note that the last digit of any number is always punched in the last column of that assigned word; blanks are left at the beginning of a 10-digit word rather than at the end.

STORAGE

The heart of a computer lies in its storage unit. There are many kinds of storage devices—magnetic drums, magnetic disks, magnetic tapes, electronic tubes, thin film—but we shall give IMCOM magnetic cores, an increasingly popular storage device used in modern computers.

Although the actual operation of magnetic core storage is somewhat complicated, all we need to know is that these cores, tiny doughnut-shaped rings about the size of a pinhead, have the same storage characteristics as other storage devices: they can store only two values, 1 or 0. All cores have a value of 0 until they have been changed to a value of 1. This counting method, then, goes back to our previous discussion of binary numbers and the binary-decimal system (see pp. 92–97).

With six cores placed directly below each other, IMCOM has the capacity to record any number, 0–9, merely by placing electric

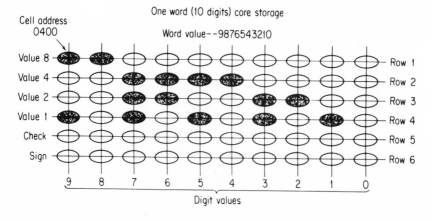

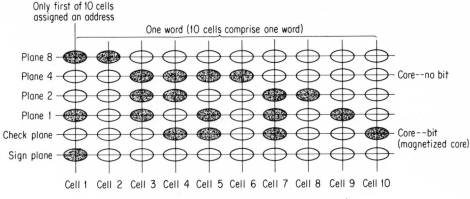

Only first of 10 cells assigned an address

One word (10 cells comprise one word)

Plane 8

Plane 4 — Core--no bit

Plane 2

Plane 1

Check plane — Core--bit (magnetized core)

Sign plane

Cell 1 Cell 2 Cell 3 Cell 4 Cell 5 Cell 6 Cell 7 Cell 8 Cell 9 Cell 10

(Each cell comprised of 6 cores directly below each other)

charges in the proper cores. Actually, only four cores are necessary; but we shall use six in IMCOM for reasons to be explained later. If IMCOM read the 10-digit word of 9876543210 from a data card, each of the ten digits in the word would be represented by the appropriate "charged" cores.

Six cores placed directly below each other are called a *cell*. In the following illustration, the first cell of the ten would have an address representing all 10 cells comprising one single word (illustration shows a 10-digit word stored in address 0400). Therefore, 10 cells are needed to represent the one word shown in the illustration, but only one cell, the first, would be assigned an address number.

Assume that IMCOM has a 2,000-word capacity. As just noted, each word requires that one cell address be assigned for all 10 cells. *All* IMCOM words must contain 10 digits (see p. 146). Therefore, if we assume that IMCOM has a storage capacity of 2,000 words and if each word requires 10 digits, IMCOM would have facilities for 20,000 digits.

> 2,000 words
> $\times$ 10 digits per word (cells)
> 20,000 digits in storage structure

The fifth row of cores in the digits or cells is called a *check* row and is designed as a mechanical check of the computer—the programmer or computer operator need not be concerned with this checking element. Any time a core in a cell contains a "one" value,

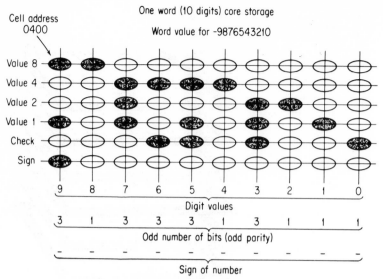

Cell address 0400

One word (10 digits) core storage

Word value for -9876543210

Value 8 · Value 4 · Value 2 · Value 1 · Check · Sign

9 8 7 6 5 4 3 2 1 0

Digit values

3 1 3 3 3 1 3 1 1 1

Odd number of bits (odd parity)

Sign of number

it is said to contain a *bit*; if the core contains a "zero" value, it has no bit. Computers are built to test themselves to see whether they have an odd number of bits or an even number of bits in each cell. The computer does not care in what rows the bits are recorded; it is interested only in how many bits have been recorded in each cell. If a computer is required always to have an odd number of bits per cell, it has been built on an *odd parity*. If it must always have an even number of bits per cell, it has been built on an *even parity*. IMCOM was built on an odd parity; therefore, each cell must contain an odd total of bits within its six rows of cores. It must have either one, three, or five bits for each cell. If it does not, the computer will stop operations because it knows something is wrong with its mechanical parts. That is what parity is for—to check the operation of the computer's components.

Notice in the preceding illustration that a check bit was needed in the cells containing the numbers 6, 5, 3, and 0. If a check bit had not been placed in the cells of these four numbers, there would have been an even number of bits in each cell (two bits in 6, two bits in 5, two bits in 3, and zero bits in 0), and the computer would not accept these digits during processing operations.

Notice, too, that the bottom level of cores (Row 6) contains a sign bit in the cell containing the first digit, number 9. This one sign bit will transform the positive number of 10 digits into a negative number: —9876543210. If no bit is present in the sign row of the first cell of a 10-digit number, the number is assumed to be positive.

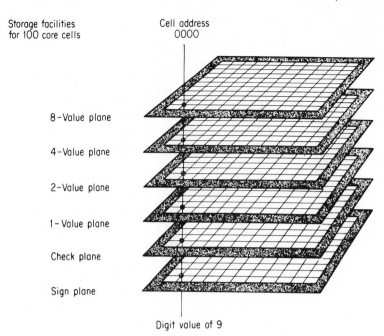

Storage facilities
for 100 core cells

Cell address
0000

8-Value plane

4-Value plane

2-Value plane

1-Value plane

Check plane

Sign plane

Digit value of 9

The foregoing illustration shows only 10 cells composed of 6 rows or what are called *planes*. In actual computer storage, each plane is a square in which 100 wires from each side intersect (rather than the 10 wires illustrated); and a core is placed around each intersection of the wires.

Only the top plane receives a cell address; the five planes below, however, are necessary for storing any number. When IMCOM reads out the number in Address 0000, it will come to the location of intersecting wires identified as 0000 and then read the top plane and each intersecting wire in the five planes below it. If we had 100 wires from each side, we would have 100 $\times$ 100 or 10,000 cells.

From the previous illustration, it is possible to see how a numeric value (a value of 9) is stored at a specified address (Address 0000). In addition to showing only 100 cells instead of the true 10,000, the diagram shows only the first digit of a word. Remember, each word in IMCOM's storage is made up of 10 digits. When we ask IMCOM to read the word stored in Address 0000, it will read us the value contained in 10 consecutive cells starting at 0000 and ending 10 cells later at 0001. The illustration, therefore, actually shows a value of a word at 0000 as 90000000000.

We are now getting involved in one of the more difficult elements of programming: placing instructions and data in storage at specific addresses and keeping track of where instructions and data have been stored. Assume that, of the 2,000 word addresses available for storage in IMCOM, Addresses 0400–0699 are reserved for storage of instructions; Addresses 0700–1199 are used for storage of input data; and Addresses 1200–2000 are used for storage of processed data. In our payroll problem, Addresses 0001–0399 will be left unassigned. The numbers to keep in mind when writing our program are as follows:

> Addresses 0400–0699: instruction storage
> Addresses 0700–1199: data storage
> Addresses 1200–2000: temporary storage

The first card read by IMCOM, the card which tells it that the following cards are instruction cards, will tell IMCOM to begin placing the instruction information at Addresses 0400. Remember, only 10 digits (one word) are punched into each instruction card. When the second 10-digit instruction card is read, the contents of that card will be placed in the next 10-cell storage space, or in Address 0401. When all the instruction cards have been read into storage (there will be 24 instruction cards in the program as illustrated on p. 152), the special card that follows the program deck will tell IMCOM that the stored program is now complete and that IMCOM is to go to Address 0400 to read and execute the first of the stored instructions.

When IMCOM goes to Address 0400, the instruction in that address will tell IMCOM to read in a card, the first data card involved in the processing. This first card contains several constant numbers that will be used during the processing of each payroll card. For example, a constant number of 40 must be used for each employee's pay calculation because we must know for overtime pay calculation whether the employee worked less than 40 hours, exactly 40 hours, or more than 40 hours. This constant value of 40 will be subtracted from the number of hours worked for each employee. Thus this constant value of 40 and other numbers of similar type must be placed in storage before they can be used.

After these constants are placed in storage in addresses starting at 0900, the next instruction, that in Address 0401, will tell IM-COM to read in a variable payroll data card containing the employee's identification number, total hours worked, hourly wage rate, tax withheld, and other deductions. Data from this first employee card will be placed in Addresses 0700 (employee number), 0701 (total hours worked), 0702 (hourly wage rate), 0703 (Federal income tax withheld), and 0704 (total other deductions). Each data card will contain these same five words; therefore, we must plan to store these five words in five data storage addresses: Addresses 0700–0704.

Let us run through the computation previously discussed (pp. 133–36). We shall call our first employee "Employee 8." Employee 8 has the following data:

Employee number	8
Total hours worked	44
Hourly wage rate	$5.00
Federal income tax withheld	$26.00
Total other deductions	$9.50

The foregoing data punched into a punched card will appear as follows:

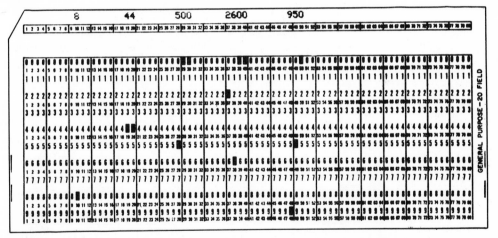

The data taken from the punched card will be placed in consecutive data addresses starting at Address 0700, as directed in Instruction 2 of the program shown earlier (p. 182). The Hollerith code used to register data in our punched cards is not the binary-decimal code used by IMCOM to store figures; therefore, before IMCOM places any data in its storage cells, it must translate the punched card code into the binary-decimal code. After the data is stored in the cells using the binary-decimal code (see pp. 156–59), the cells in the storage unit of IMCOM will be as shown on p. 162.

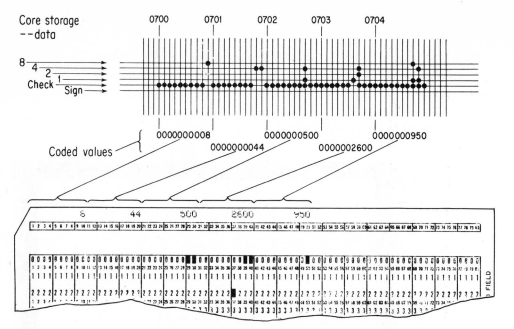

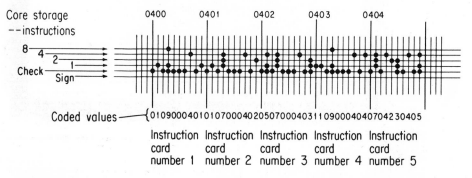

The cells assigned for instruction storage, Addresses 0400–0699, would appear as follows for the first five instructions.

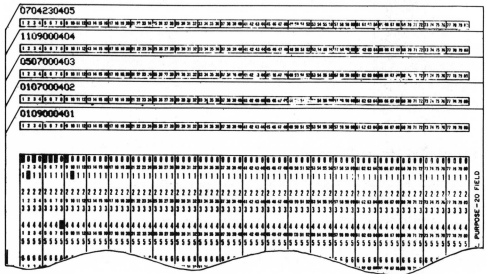

Notice that throughout the discussion of computers we have used the term *storage* rather than the term *memory*. Memory implies a degree of thinking ability; IMCOM, like other computers, cannot think. It can only store data; it cannot memorize data.

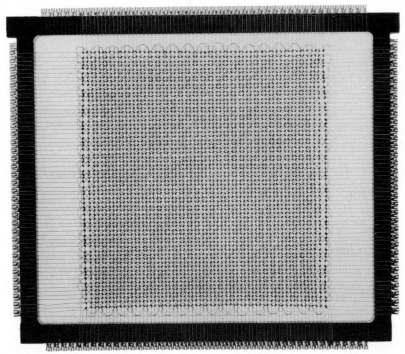

Courtesy of the IBM Corporation.

A plane of magnetic cores.

As just noted, IMCOM's storage facilities consist of magnetic cores, small metallic doughnuts strung on wires. Such core storage has many advantages and is a very common storage media in actual computers now in use; but other types of storage devices are also used in today's computers.

Magnetic Drum Storage

Most storage devices follow the two-stage principle (on-off or magnetized-nonmagnetized stage) similar to that just described in discussing IMCOM's storage facility. One of the first storage devices used in early computers was the magnetic drum, a steel cylinder coated with a metallic material capable of receiving and storing

Magnetic drum storage unit.

electronic charges. The drum storage device is still used in modern computers; it is, however, more frequently used as the main storage device in small computers and as an extra or auxiliary storage device in large computers. In large computers, data may be stored on the slower drums and then transferred to the faster cores just before the data is actually used during the processing of the program. The storage unit of a large computer may be made up of a combination of core, drum, disk, or other storage devices.

While the drum turns at a very rapid and constant speed (up to 15,000 revolutions per minute), its surface passes under "read-write" heads which can record data on the drum surface or read data off the drum. Recording data on the drum is basically the same process as recording it on magnetic tape (see pp. 114–16).

Just as the bits in IMCOM's cores are combined to represent

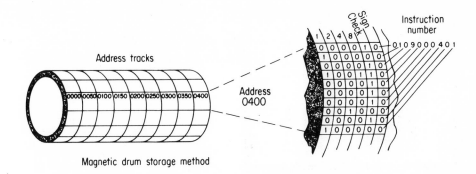

Magnetic drum storage method

numbers, the bits recorded on the drum are also recorded as codes and are later interpreted as numbers or letters. If, for example, the address of 0400 was to contain the first 10-digit instruction for our payroll problem, the bits recorded on the drum would also be recorded as codes. When that address was located during the processing of the program, the read-write heads above the channel or band containing the numbers in Address 0400 would read the codes off the drum and send the numbered instructions to the control unit for processing. The processing of the payroll would be identical to that of IMCOM; only the storage media has been changed.

Magnetic Disk Storage

Another storage method commonly used in modern computers is the disk or "juke-box" device. This device consists of several "records" or disks which resemble phonograph records except that they are grooveless metal disks coated with a ferrous oxide metal similar to that used on magnetic drums and capable of receiving and storing electronic charges. Several disks are placed permanently on a spindle to make up a unit looking much like a stack of records stored in a juke-box. The disks are slightly separated so that an access arm similar to a juke-box tone arm can be moved above a specified disk and thus place new data on the disk or read previously stored data off the disk. In such a storage device, the disks cannot be removed; the access arm must slide up and down a rod to locate a specified disk before the read-write head can be moved to the proper place above the disk. A relatively new modification of disk storage is the *disk pack*, a group of six disks, each disk having its own read-write head, thus eliminating the time necessary for the access arm to move up and down the rod to locate the desired

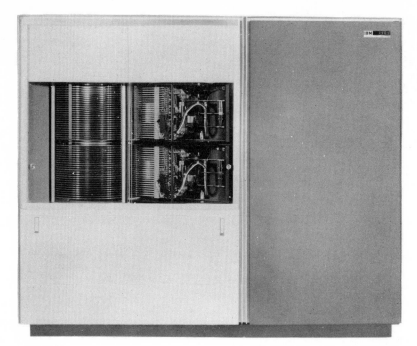

Magnetic disk storage unit.

disk. Unlike the disks in the standard disk storage device that resembles the juke-box, the six disks in a disk pack can be removed as a complete unit and another unit of six disks placed in the disk-pack unit.

The principles of magnetic disk storage are very similar to the method of storing data on a magnetc drum. Like the drums, the disks receive electronic impulses from read-write heads in the form of codes. Instead of one continuous recording groove as on a phonograph record, each disk has as many as 500 separate tracks similar to the channels or bands on a magnetic drum. As the disk rotates at speeds near 1,500 revolutions per minute, the access arm locates the proper disk and moves in far enough to permit the read-write head to be positioned directly over one specific track on the disk. Each track or channel is separate from any other and the read-write head must move again to record or extract other data from another track. Data is thus stored or obtained by knowing the address of the desired data, locating the disk containing that address, moving the access arm with the read-write head directly over the proper track, and reading or writing the data in a specified section of that selected track.

Disk-pack storage unit.

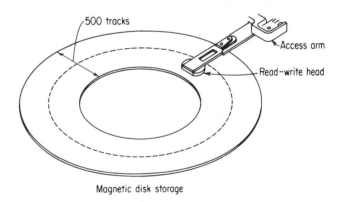

Magnetic disk storage

Magnetic Card Storage

Still another storage media used in computers and becoming increasingly popular is the magnetic card, sometimes referred to as a *strip* or a *belt*. In theory, recording data on the magnetic card is the same as recording it on magnetic tape, magnetic drum, or magnetic disk. A metallic coating on each card is capable of receiving and storing electronic impulses.

Data cell storage unit.

Many cards are placed inside metal containers called *data cells* or *cartridges*. Computer manufacturers have developed different methods for mechanically retrieving any one specified card from the container. After the proper card has been located and taken from the container, it is wrapped around a revolving cylinder which passes a read-write head as it revolves—the card device is now mechanically similar in operation to a revolving magnetic drum. After the card has passed the read-write head and the data has been recorded on or taken off the card, the card is released from the drum and returned to the container.

Each card has several tracks on its surface as if several sections of magnetic tape had been cut and stuck on a card. And, like the magnetic drum and magnetic disk, read-write heads are positioned over the proper tracks when the desired data is recorded or extracted from the card. After the card has been processed, it is released from the revolving drum and returns to the container.

Magnetic core, drum, disk, or card storage are all considered as random storage devices because they can provide addressed locations with limited searching. Magnetic tapes, on the other hand, are sequential storage devices which require searching each preceding record before the next record is read. If a tape contained 100,000 records and record 99,999 was needed, each of the 99,998 records would be analyzed before arriving at record 99,999.

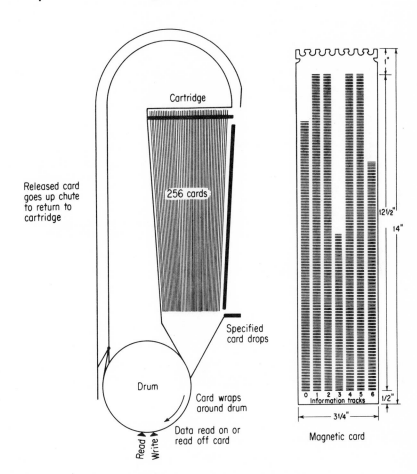

Because the drum, disk, or card may have to make almost one revolution (if the read-write head has just passed the addressed location), core storage is the most truly random storage device because the control goes directly to the addressed location and is totally independent of any other address location; searching is eliminated. This feature of true random selection of addresses makes core storage much faster than drum, disk, or card; but the random selection feature of core storage also limits the amount of storage addresses available within a computer and increases the cost much above drum, disk, or card storage devices.

CONTROL UNIT

Up to now, we have seen how a computer can receive and store both instructions and data in a binary-decimal code within its storage facilities. We have noted that the instructions are fed into the storage unit through the input media of punched cards and are expressed as digits representing the operations that the computer is to perform. These numeric codes are the same as the plus bar, minus bar, multiplication bar, and other operation keys found on the keyboard of a deck calculator. But the computer has many more of these automatic operations built into it than a desk calculator; by using numeric codes, the computer requires no human activity to perform the operations.

But if the storage unit is used only for storage, how, then, does the computer know when to execute specific instructions containing specific data? What makes the whole thing tick?

Equivalent to the person sitting behind the desk calculator is the *control unit* within the computer. The control unit is the "overseer" or master of everything that happens in all the computer units. The information stored in a computer's storage unit in the computer's language can be moved around, cut in pieces, assembled, disassembled, or handled in a variety of ways—all at the direction of the control unit. The person is the true boss; the control unit is our foreman; the other computer units are our workers.

The instructions written for the computer must be properly coded into the computer's language so that the control unit can follow the instructions automatically and in the desired sequence. It is the control unit that decodes the various numeric instructions it obtains from storage and sets the proper circuitry to work to perform the specified instructions. To see how the control unit of IMCOM would function, let's examine the instructions of our payroll problem as shown earlier (see p. 152).

When the special card inserted after the instruction deck tells IMCOM to begin processing the payroll data, IMCOM will automatically shift control to the control unit. The entire 10-digit word comprising the first instruction and stored in Address 0400 will be called for by the control unit for examination and execution. When the control unit gets this word from storage, the word 0109000401, the control unit will analyze the first two digits to determine what action it must tell other units of IMCOM to perform. Remember, all our instructions follow the same format. Therefore, IMCOM

10-digit computer word

1	2	3	4	5	6	7	8	9	10
x	x	x	x	x	x	x	x	x	x

Opera-tion code	Data address	Instruction address

always knows to look at the first two digits to determine what operation is to be performed; to look at the next four digits to determine where to find the data upon which the operation will be performed; and to look at the last four digits to determine where to go to get the next instruction that is to be analyzed. When the control unit reads the first instruction and finds the code 01 as the first two numbers in the word 0109000401, it will recognize this code to mean "Read a card." IMCOM has been built to understand that when the code "01" is interpreted, the control unit relays a message to the input unit telling input to read in the data contained on the next punched card. In addition to communicating with the input unit, the control unit will also tell the storage unit to accept the data that input is going to give it and to place this data in a specific storage address—in this instruction the address is 0900.

Because there are 80 columns of digits on a punched card, and each word is 10 digits long, each card contains 8 words and thus requires 8 addresses. A command, such as "Read a card," means to store the first word of 10 digits, then store the second word on the card, then the third word, and so on, until the 8 words on the card have been stored in 8 consecutive addresses, the first of which was designated in the instruction. The illustration (p. 162) shows data stored after one punched card has been read. Only 5 of the 8 possible words were punched into the employee cards in our payroll problem. If more than 8 words are required to put data into storage before the calculations begin, the next card will also be read and the contents placed in storage starting at Address 0908, and so on. The storage of data always begins at the address stated in the instruction: Address 0900 in our first instruction for processing our payroll.

After the control unit has told the input unit to read in a card and has told the storage unit to accept this information and place it in a specified address, the control unit immediately tells storage to send the 10-digit word called for in the last four digits of the number it has analyzed. The 0401 that has been called for from storage by the control unit will replace the previous 10-digit word that has been executed. A call for a new word automatically erases the preceding word in the control unit. Even though the words are sent from storage to the control unit to be analyzed, the words remain in storage exactly as they were entered. Nothing is removed from storage when the control unit calls for a new word; only a "duplicate" of the stored word is sent to control.

Thanks to the control unit of IMCOM, our computer now knows through our written instructions stored within IMCOM just where to locate the numbers to be used in a certain command that we have ordered, and where to go to get the next instruction to be executed. Our foreman, the control unit, is now running the show.

ARITHMETIC UNIT

In addition to the input unit, the storage unit, and the control unit, IMCOM, like all other electronic computers, also has an arithmetic unit. The input unit gives adequate instructions and data to be stored while awaiting a call from the control unit. The control unit calls for data from storage and places the data in the central processing unit, the arithmetic unit, where the data is manipulated in a predetermined manner. This arithmetic unit performs such operations as arithmetic (add, subtract, multiply, and divide), shifting, transferring, comparing, and other simple operations involving numbers.

The arithmetic unit is comprised of a varying number of *registers*. Large expensive computers contain many registers; small computers have only a few because the automatic operations are more limited. Basically, a register can receive, hold, or transfer data as directed by the control unit; it can temporarily store data before, during, and after an operation. A register's function is similar to the dials that indicate the numbers being processed in a desk calculator and to the gears and wheels that actually do the calculating in a desk calculator. An arithmetic unit often contains one register for each defined function: an add-substract register accepts, adds, or subtracts data; a multiplication register processes data when the multiplication function is needed; a division register divides data; a storage register temporarily holds data in the arithmetic unit rather than return it to the main storage unit, and so on.

When we operate a desk calculator, we do not attempt to understand "why" it computes as it does; the inner workings of wheels, gears, nuts, and bolts are of no interest to us. We only want the answers. The same thing is true of computers. To simplify our understanding of computer operations, we will assume IMCOM has only one register, and this register will perform all of IMCOM's arithmetic and logic operations. We should know that registers do exist in computers; we need not know how each register works. For example, it is much easier to understand that the register in IMCOM actually stores data in the arithmetic unit. When the control unit attempts to execute a command of "05" or "RLR" (reset and load the register), the control unit sends a figure from storage to the arithmetic unit. This figure from storage is then placed in the temporary storage facility in the arithmetic unit, or the register, awaiting further processing. The control unit may then execute a "10" or "ADD" operation in which a figure from the main storage unit is located and sent to the arithmetic unit where the figure is added to the value already in storage in the register. The answer obtained from the addition of these two figures remains in temporary storage in the register until it is commanded to place the answer somewhere in the main storage unit. The important point to remember is that the register is like the dials of a desk calculator; it will continue to hold new answers of as many operations as we wish, and it will not clear itself until it is told to do so. If we place the number 4 in the register, add the number 10 in the next operation, then subtract 2, and then divide by 3, the register will contain a new answer after each operation (4, then 14, then 12, and then 4) and will hold the final answer of 4 after the last operation has been completed.

Again remember that sending data to the arithmetic unit does not destroy the data in the main storage unit from which it was sent. Only a "duplicate" of the stored data goes to the arithmetic unit for processing; the original data remains in storage. But, and this, too, is important, when new or different data is placed in a storage address, the new data replaces the old data in storage. In other words, data taken from storage does not change the data in storage; but data returned to, or originally placed in, storage replaces the figures in that particular cell or address. For example, let's assume that cell Address 1201 contains the figure 0000003000. When the control unit calls for this figure to be placed in the arithmetic unit for addition to another number, Address 1201 still contains the value of 0000003000 even though it has sent that value to the arithmetic unit. Numbers taken from storage do not destroy those numbers held in storage. Assume the control unit later tells the arithmetic unit to store an answer of 0000019450 in Address 1201. At the command "06" or "STR," the number contained in Address 1201 is automatically erased, Address 1201 is cleared, and the number 0000019450 is placed in Address 1201. Numbers placed into storage replace the numbers that were formerly in the storage addresses.

OUTPUT UNIT

After the data has been completely processed and the results placed in proper storage addresses, the control unit orders the output unit to communicate the data in an understandable form to the persons desiring the information. This communication can be done through a direct printout of the data by an electric typewriter or by a line printer, both of which are connected directly to the computer. The typewriter or the printer receives the data that was in selected storage addresses and that has been translated into the English language and then produces a *hard copy*, a printed listing of the data resulting from the processing performed by the computer's units. Of the two print-out media, the typewriter is the slower method of producing hard copy since it prints at only 120 words per minute. Some line printers can produce copy at the rate of 34,000 words per minute—a speed ridiculously slow when compared to the processing speed in terms of millionths of one second performed within the computer's processing components.

A great deal of the output function is in the form of an indirect medium in which additional processing is necessary on auxiliary equipment not directly connected to the computer. Examples of indirect output media are magnetic tape, punched tape, and punched cards. If huge volumes of data must be stored, magnetic tape is generally used. Punched tape and punched cards do not have magnetic tape's density advantage for storage; punched cards, however, have a distinct advantage in that the sequence of cards may rather easily be altered whenever the need arises. Punched cards are popular as an output medium because it is easy to handle the cards when considerable handling of the data is necessary after processing has been completed.

We shall assume that IMCOM will provide its output information through punched cards. As may be noted in Instruction 23 of the payroll problem programmed earlier (p. 152), after the net pay of one employee has been computed and the figure placed in storage next to the empoyee's name (Addresses 1200 and 1201), a command is given to "02" PCH (punch a card) containing the two stored values: (1) the employee's identification number held in Address 1200, (2) the employee's net pay held in Address 1201. The program then informs the control unit to go back to the beginning of the processing (Instruction 2), read in a new card containing the pertinent data of another employee, and process that new data.

When all the data cards have been processed, the output unit will hold one punched card for each data card that was passed through the input unit and the contents placed in storage for processing. The punched cards will then be taken from the output unit, placed in an auxiliary printer when a listing of the data is desired, and the data contained on each card (employee number and the net pay) will be printed in a listed form. The desired spacing between the employee identification number and the net pay due can be regulated by the board wiring within the printer. An example of the output for our payroll is shown. Our first employee, Employee Number 8, will be paid $194.50; the card will not contain printed data at the top but only punched coded data.

SUMMARY

Now that we have developed a new friendship with our helper, IMCOM, let's return, look behind its face, and review what makes IMCOM tick.

We have seen that IMCOM employs a binary type of machine language represented by two possible values, a 1 value or a 0 value, and the position in which the 1 values are placed indicates the decimal value of numbers which we can understand. IMCOM will accept only numbers rather than letters; it is not as versatile as some of the very large computers. IMCOM is so fussy that we must always feed it only 10-digit words. But once IMCOM receives our 10-digit words, it can manipulate the words in terms of predetermined sequences of operations stated in a program that IMCOM has placed in its storage facilities. Within this program are the routines and blocks of instructions that complete the desired arithmetic computations and permit simple comparisons necessary for making yes-no decisions.

We have noted that the basic idea behind IMCOM is its ability to store both data and instructions. Although the computer storage principle resembles the method of storing mail in post office mail boxes, the analogy does fail in two respects: (1) only one piece of communication (word) can be stored in any one designated address; (2) the data still remains in the addressed location even when the stored data is used. But however complex a data processing

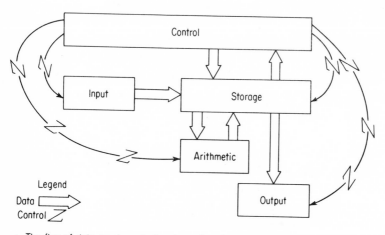

The flow of data, as shown in the above chart, is as follows:
1. Data and instructions are placed into storage through the input unit.
2. The first instruction moves from storage to control.

problem, the basic theroy of computer operations remains the same; both the data and the instructions are fed into the computer's storage through the input unit, and the control unit takes over from there as it follows the stored instructions.

The flow of data, as shown in the foregoing chart, is as follows:

1. Data and instructions are placed into storage through the input unit.

2. The first instruction moves from storage to control.

3. The control unit analyzes the instruction to
   Determine what operation must be performed.
   Determine where to go in storage to get the next instruction.

4. The control unit sends a signal to storage telling it to send a number in a specified address to the arithmetic unit.

5. The control unit then tells the arithmetic unit to perform a specific arithmetic or logic function.

6. The control unit then commands the arithmetic unit to place the results of the arithmetic or logic function in a designated address in storage.

7. The control unit then informs the storage unit to send the data contained in designated addresses to the output unit for print-out or punch-out.

Some basic characteristics of the five components that make up our computer are as follows:

Input unit	Input feeds in data only when directed to do so.
	All data must go directly to storage.
	Input will accept data in a different code but will translate it into its own computer language.
Storage unit	Storage supplies the data and instructions during processing and furnishes the results to output.

Each storage facility has an assigned address number.

Stored information can be referred to once or as many times as desired.

Stored information can be replaced whenever desired.

Information sent to other units remains unaltered in the storage address from which it was sent.

All data must pass through the storage unit.

Control unit

All computer units operate under the direction of the control unit.

All instructions are decoded and interpreted in the control unit.

Instructions are available to the control unit as they are needed to direct the specified sequence.

Arithmetic unit

The four arithmetic operations are performed, numbers are shifted and compared, and simple logical decisions are made.

Data is temporarily stored and computed in registers.

Data may be transferred to other units of the computer.

Output unit

Output data must come from storage unit.

Output data may be printed or typed in direct copy from high-speed printer or electric typewriter; or may be indirect copy in media of punched cards, punched tapes, or magnetic tapes.

A computer system, then, is made up of the five components discussed before. IMCOM has served as a representative computer incorporating many of the important characteristics common to each of these five units. Actually, we barely scratched the surface of the subject of computers in terms of the capabilities of each unit. With the rapid advances being made in the development of computer equipment and technology, it would not be feasible to delve too deeply into the minute working elements of any specific type of computer. By now some the mystery of electronic computers should have faded and been replaced by a general understanding of what an electronic computer system is all about.

This amazing product of modern science is only beginning to find its place in the data processing field. The practical uses of computers in business are becoming more and more apparent. A careful examination of actual processing operations being performed in business by electronic computers will show that the basic steps previously done by people on typewriters and desk calculators are incorporated in the processing being performed by the electronic computers. As noted on p. 180, there are some differences in the basic operations of desk calculators and computers; if, however, we consider the control unit as a person, the method and sequence of data processing by computers are quite similar to the manual operations performed before computers were introduced.

The program for our payroll problem (p. 182) and the detailed explanations of each instruction shown (pp. 183–193) are presented as a review of the basic operations of a computer. This program, once formulated, tried, and approved, would be the same program used each week for the computation of the weekly payroll. Only the data recorded on the data cards would be handled by the clerical staff. So with the proper instructions being used over and over again, we would eliminate much of the error attributable to the human element; and we would have the benefits of increased processing speed and decreased clerical cost. It is no wonder that some authors have compared the electronic computer to a highly regimented force.

> . . . the machine might be, and has sometimes been equated to legions—an army, if you will—of low-grade morons whose conceptualization is entirely literal, who remember as long as is necessary or as you desire them to, whose loyalty and subservience is complete, who require no holidays, no spurious incentives, no morale programs, pensions, not even gratitude for past service, and who seemingly never tire of doing elementary tasks, such as typing, accounting, bookkeeping, arithmetic, filling in forms, and the like.*

* Roger Nett and Stanley A. Hetzler, *An Introduction to Electronic Data Processing* (Glencoe, Ill.: The Free Press, 1959), pp. 87-8.

COMPARISON OF DESK CALCULATOR AND COMPUTER

Desk Calculator	Computer
Input	
Keys depressed on keyboard.	Input automatically fed to storage by punched cards or tapes, magnetic tapes, scanning devices, or electric typewriter.
No preprocessing of data required.	Preprocessing of data required.
Storage	
No prestored instructions.	Prestored instructions necessary to execute desired functions.
Operation button selected by operator.	No separate selections necessary.
Sequence determined by operator.	Sequence predetermined in rigid form.
Stored data generally not a function.	Stored data consists of thousands of digits.
Data retained on paper or in mind of operator.	
Data lost when calculations occur.	Data retained in storage unit.
Control	
Operations selected by operator.	Operations determined from stored instructions.
Arithmetic	
Button or operation bar depressed to activate computations.	Reading and executing operation code by control unit activates computations.
Dials and gears move to perform computations.	Electronic pulses within special registers perform computations.
Limited number of automatic operations available	Many automatic operations coded and built into computer.
Dials reveal results.	Registers temporarily hold results.
Output	
Visual reading of dials.	Direct printout of answers or indirect coded media for later printout.

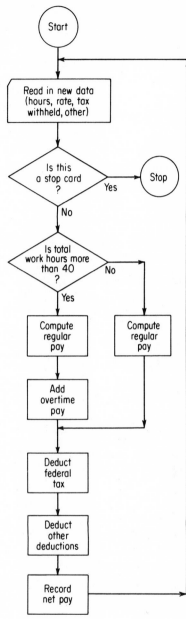

Block diagram representation of the payroll problem.

MODEL PROGRAM FOR PAYROLL PROBLEM

Mnemonic Aid	Opera-tion Code	English Translation	Data Storage Addresses	
RDC	01	Read a card	0700	Employee number
PCH	02	Punch a card	0701	Total hours worked
SHR	03	Shift to right	0702	Hourly wage rate
SHL	04	Shift to left	0703	Federal income tax
RLR	05	Reset and load register		withheld
STR	06	Store	0704	Total other deductions
BRP	07	Branch on positive		
BRN	08	Branch on negative	0900	Constant value -- 10,000
HLT	09	Halt operations	0901	Constant value -- 40
ADD	10	Add	0902	Constant value -- 1.5
SUB	11	Subtract		
MUL	12	Multiply		
DIV	13	Divide	Last Card (Dummy) Employee Number -- 12,000	

PROBLEM: PAYROLL FOR IMCOM   WRITTEN BY: Langenbach

INSTR NO.	LOCATION OF INSTR	OPERATION ABBRV	CODE	ADDRESS DATA	INSTR	REMARKS
1	0400	RDC	01	0900	0401	Read constants into addresses 0900-0907
2	0401	RDC	01	0700	0402	Read Employee data into addresses 0700-0707
3	0402	RLR	05	0700	0403	Reset register to 0; load in Empl. no. from 0700
4	0403	SUB	11	0900	0404	Subtract no. in 0900 (10,000) from Empl. no.
5	0404	BRP	07	0423	0405	If answer is +, go to 0423; if – or 0, go to 0405
6	0405	ADD	10	0900	0406	Add back 0900 (10,000) to restore Empl. no.
7	0406	STR	06	1200	0407	Store Empl. no. in address 1200
8	0407	RLR	05	0701	0408	Reset register to 0, load in hrs. worked (0701)
9	0408	SUB	11	0901	0409	Subtract 0901 (40) from hrs. worked
10	0409	BRP	07	0412	0410	If answer is + (more than 40 hrs) go to 0412; if answer is – or 0 (less or equal to 40 hrs) go to 0410
11	0410	ADD	10	0901	0411	Add back 0901 (40) to restore hrs. worked
12	0411	MUL	12	0702	0419	Multiply total hours by hourly rate (0702)
13	0412	MUL	12	0902	0413	Multiply overtime hrs. by 1½ (0902)
14	0413	MUL	12	0702	0414	Multiply total overtime hrs. by hourly wage rate
15	0414	SHR	03	0001	0415	Shift answer 1 place to right to compensate for fraction in Instruction 0412
16	0415	STR	06	1201	0416	Store overtime pay in 1201
17	0416	RLR	05	0901	0417	Reset register to 0; load regular hrs. of 40 (0901)
18	0417	MUL	12	0702	0418	Multiply regular hrs. (40) by hourly rate (0702)
19	0418	ADD	10	1201	0419	Add overtime to regular pay to get gross pay
20	0419	SUB	11	0703	0420	Subtract Federal income tax withheld
21	0420	SUB	11	0704	0421	Subtract total other deductions
22	0421	STR	06	1201	0422	Store net pay in Address 1201
23	0422	PCH	02	1200	0401	Punch a card with stored Empl. no. (1200) and net pay (1201); return to address 0401
24	0423	HLT	09	0000	0000	Halt operations

EXPLANATION OF MODEL PROGRAM FOR PAYROLL PROBLEM ON IMCOM

The first data card to be read will contain three constant num-bers—numbers whose values remain the same throughout the pro-cessing of the program. The card containing these three numbers will be read in only once; therefore, it is placed ahead of the employee data cards to be processed later, one at a time. The numbers

Instruction number	Instruction location	Operation abbreviation	Operation code	Data address	Instruction address	Translation
1	0400	RDC	01	0900	0401	Read a card

on this first card will be stored in Addresses 0900, 0901, and 0902; they represent a search value (10,000), the numbers of hours in a regular work week (40), and the ratio allowed for overtime pay (1½). These three numbers are stored in addresses beyond the locations assigned to data for individual employee payroll data.

Constant card computation

Address 0900—0000010000 (search value of 10,000)

Address 0901—0000000040 (hours in regular work week—40)

Address 0902—0000000015 (ratio for overtime: 1.5)

Instruction number	Instruction location	Operation abbreviation	Operation code	Data address	Instruction address	Translation
2	0401	RDC	01	0700	0402	Read a card

The data on the employee payroll card is read by the input unit; the data of five words is stored in five addresses starting at 0700—0700—employee number; 0701—total hours worked; 0702—hourly wage rate; 0703—federal income tax withheld; 0704—total other deductions. After the five words are stored, the control unit calls in the instruction from Address 0402 for analysis and execution.

Computation on first employee

Address 0700—0000000008 (employee number—8)

Address 0701—0000000044 (total hours worked—44)

Address 0702—0000000500 (hourly wage rate—$5.00)

Address 0703—0000002600 (Federal income tax—$26.00)

Address 0704—0000000950 (total other deductions—$9.50)

Instruction number	Instruction location	Operation abbreviation	Operation code	Data address	Instruction address	Translation
3	0402	RLR	05	0700	0403	Reset and load register

When the operation code 05 is interpreted, any figures contained in the register of the arithmetic unit are erased, and the register is set to 0000000000. The register is then loaded with the employee's identification number previously stored in Address 0700. The control unit then calls for the next instruction from Address 0403.

Computation on first employee

The number 0000000008 (employee identification number 8) is placed in the register after the register's storage has been set to zero (0000000000).

Instruction number	Instruction location	Operation abbreviation	Operation code	Data address	Instruction address	Translation
4	0403	SUB	11	0900	0404	Subtract

The number stored in Address 0900 (the constant value of 10,000) is sent from storage to the arithmetic unit where it is subtracted from the employee identification number placed in the register by the previous instruction. The answer is then retained in the register. The instruction contained in Address 0404 is then called to the control unit for analysis.

Computations on first employee

The number 0000010000 (10,000) is subtracted from the employee number 0000000008 (8); the answer is temporarily stored in the register; answer is −9999990008.

Instruction number	Instruction location	Operation abbreviation	Operation code	Data address	Instruction address	Translation
5	0404	BRP	07	0423	0405	Branch on positive

If the answer obtained from subtracting 0000010000 (10,000) from the employee number 0000000008 (8) is positive (employee number is larger than 10,000), the next instruction to be analyzed will come from the address shown in the Data Address, Address 0423. The instruction in 0423 is a command to stop operations. To have the control go to 0423 because of a positive number as the answer, a special "termination" card containing an artificial employee number greater than 10,000 will be placed at the end of the employee data deck. When this card with the artificial number of 12,000 is used, a plus number will result when the constant 10,000 is subtracted from it; and a branch to instruction 0423 will halt the processing. Thus all actual employee numbers must be 10,000 or less. Notice that the data address is also used as an instruction address in this branching operation. If the answer after subtraction of 10,000 is 0 or a minus number, the instruction from Address 0405 will be called into the control unit for analysis.

Computation on first employee

The subtraction in the previous instruction resulted in a negative number $(8 - 10,000)$; therefore, the next instruction to be interpreted will come from Address 0405.

Instruction number	Instruction location	Operation abbreviation	Operation code	Data address	Instruction address	Translation
6	0405	ADD	10	0900	0406	Add

When a minus or 0 number results from the subtraction of 0000010000 (10,000), the number of 10,000 as contained in Address 0900 is added back to the negative number being held in the register. The new answer will be the employee's true identification number. The addition of 10,000 merely restores the value to what it was before 10,000 was taken away. The next instruction to be analyzed is in Address 0406.

Computation on first employee

0000010000 (10,000) is added to the answer (−9999990008) with a result of 8, the employee's identification number.

Instruction number	Instruction location	Operation abbreviation	Operation code	Data address	Instruction address	Translation
7	0406	STR	06	1200	0407	Store

The employee's identification number 0000000008 (8) is stored in Address 1200. Address 1200 need not be cleared because a storing operation automatically clears the designated address before a number is placed in the storage address. A net-pay figure will later be stored in Address 1201 so that the employee's number and his net pay will be stored consecutively for punching operations. Control then calls for the instruction located in Address 0407.

Computation on first employee

The number 0000000008 (8) is stored in Address 1200.

Instruction number	Instruction location	Operation abbreviation	Operation code	Data address	Instruction address	Translation
8	0407	RLR	05	0701	0408	Reset and load register

The data in Address 0701, the total hours worked, is loaded into the register. The register is automatically cleared and set to 0000000000 before the number is loaded in. Unlike the storage addresses, any number in the register is not erased when a new number is sent to it unless it is specifically commanded to do so. Control now requests a new instruction from Address 0408.

Computation on first employee

The employee number 0000000008 (8) remaining in the register is erased, and the register is set to 0000000000. The number 0000000044 (44) representing the total hours worked for employee 8 and stored in Address 0701 is then placed in the register so it now contains 0000000044 (44).

Instruction number	Instruction location	Operation abbreviation	Operation code	Data address	Instruction address	Translation
9	0408	SUB	11	0901	0409	Subtract

The constant number stored in Address 0901, or 0000000040 (40), is entered into the arithmetic unit and subtracted from the number being held in the register. The next instruction to be analyzed by the control unit is in Address 0409.

Computation on first employee

The constant number 0000000040 (40) is subtracted from the number in the register (the numbers of hours worked by the employee) of 0000000044 (44) with a result of 0000000004 (4). $44 - 40 = 4$.

Instruction number	Instruction location	Operation abbreviation	Operation code	Data address	Instruction address	Translation
10	0409	BRP	07	0412	0410	Branch on positive

If the answer from the previous instruction (number 9) is positive (total hours worked more than 40), the control unit will skip two instructions and go to Address 0412 as stated in the data address. A positive answer symbolizes the number of hours worked in excess of the regular 40 hours, or the "overtime" hours. If the answer is minus or 0 (total hours worked 40 or less), the control unit is directed to Address 0410 for its next instruction.

Computation on first employee

Because a positive answer 0000000004 (4) resulted from the preceding operation, the next instruction will be from Address 0412.

Instruction number	Instruction location	Operation abbreviation	Operation code	Data address	Instruction address	Translation
11	0410	ADD	10	0901	0411	Add

Because a minus or 0 answer resulted from the subtraction of 0000000040 (40) in Instruction 9, the value 0000000040 (40) in Address 0901 is added back to the minus number to restore the number to the original number of total hours worked. The instruction in Address 0411 is then called into the control unit for analysis.

Computation on first employee

This operation is skipped because of a positive number resulting in Instruction 9 and direction sent to Address 0412 (Instruction 13) as directed in the preceding step.

Instruction number	Instruction location	Operation abbreviation	Operation code	Data address	Instruction address	Translation
12	0411	MUL	12	0702	0419	Multiply

The total hours worked being held in the register is to be multiplied by the employee's hourly wage rate stored in Address 0702. The resulting product is the employee's gross pay from which all his deductions are to be subtracted to arrive at his net pay. The control then skips several instructions and calls for the instruction contained in Address 0419.

Computation on first employee

This operation is skipped because of a positive number resulting from Instruction 9.

Instruction number	Instruction location	Operation abbreviation	Operation code	Data address	Instruction address	Translation
13	0412	MUL	12	0902	0413	Multiply

The hours in excess of 40, the overtime hours, are the result of the subtraction performed in Instruction 9 and are being held in the register. These overtime hours are now to be multiplied by the figure in Address 0902 which is the constant 0000000015 (15). Because the computer does not register decimal points, we supply it with the figure 15 but assume it to be 1.5. The shift operation in Instruction 15 will later eliminate the effects of one decimal point. The resulting product of this multiplication will be the total overtime hours to be credited to the employee. The next instruction will come from Address 0413.

Computation on first employee

The number of hours shown in the register, 0000000004 (4), will be multiplied by the figure in Address 0902 or 0000000015 (15); and the total overtime hours will be 0000000060 (60) but assumed to 6.0 hours.

Instruction number	Instruction location	Operation abbreviation	Operation code	Data address	Instruction address	Translation
14	0413	MUL	12	0702	0414	Multiply

The total overtime hours retained in the register are to be multiplied by the employee's hourly wage rate stored in Address 0702. The answer will be the total overtime pay. The next instruction to be analyzed by the control unit is stored in Address 0414.

Computation on first employee

The total overtime hours in the register, 0000000060 (60 or 6.0), will be multiplied by the employee's hourly wage rate or 0000000500 (500 or $5.00) to arrive at the total overtime pay of 0000030000 (30000 or $30.000).

Instruction number	Instruction location	Operation abbreviation	Operation code	Data address	Instruction address	Translation
15	0414	SHR	03	0001	0415	Shift to right

When the overtime hours were multiplied by 1.5 in Instruction 13, all the numbers in the stored word in the register were automatically moved one place to the left because of the assumed decimal point. To restore the number now contained in the register to its original position, the entire 10-digit number will be shifted one place to the right, as shown in the special instruction of 0001 under the data address. Thus one zero will be added to the left of the number and one digit will be dropped from the right. The product will then reflect no decimal influence from previous calculations. The numbers held in the register's storage remain the same; only the position has been changed by adding a digit to the left and dropping a digit on the right. The next instruction will be found in Address 0415.

Computation on first employee

The number in the register, 0000030000 (30000) will be moved one place to the right or 0000003000 (3000 or assumed $30.00).

Instruction number	Instruction location	Operation abbreviation	Operation code	Data address	Instruction address	Translation
16	0415	STR	06	1201	0416	Store

The overtime pay now in the register must be used later to be added to the regular pay for the total gross pay. But to determine the regular pay, the register will be needed for further computations; therefore, the overtime pay will be temporarily stored in Address 1201 for a later recall. When the overtime pay is placed in Address 1201, any figures contained in that address will be erased; only the overtime figure for this computation will appear in 1201. The control unit will then call for the instruction in Address 0416.

Computation on first employee

The 10 digits in Address 1201 will be set to 0000000000 (0) and the figure in the register 0000003000 (3000 or $30.00) will be placed in Address 1201.

Instruction number	Instruction location	Operation abbreviation	Operation code	Data address	Instruction address	Translation
17	0416	RLR	05	0901	0417	Reset and load register

Any figures contained in the register are erased, and the register is set to 0000000000 (0). The register is then loaded with the number contained in Address 0901, the total regular hours of 0000000040 (40). The control unit then prepares to execute Instruction 0417.

Computation on first employee

The number in the register 0000003000 (3000) is erased, the register is reset to 0000000000 (0), and the number 0000000040 (40) from Address 0901 is loaded in the register.

Instruction number	Instruction location	Operation abbreviation	Operation code	Data address	Instruction address	Translation
18	0417	MUL	12	0702	0418	Multiply

The total regular hours, 0000000040 (40), now in the register will be multiplied by the employee's hourly wage rate found in Address 0702. The product will be the total regular-time pay. The control unit will then call for the instruction in Address 0418.

Computation on first employee

The total regular hours in the register 0000000040 (40) will be multiplied by the rate in Address 0702, 0000000500 (500 or assumed $5.00) and the product in the register will be 0000020000 (20000 or assumed $200.00).

Instruction number	Instruction location	Operation abbreviation	Operation code	Data address	Instruction address	Translation
19	0418	ADD	10	1201	0419	Add

Recall that the overtime pay was previously computed and placed in Address 1201 for storage. The control unit now directs the storage unit to return the overtime pay stored in 1201 to the arithmetic unit where the overtime pay is added to the total regular pay that has been held in the register. The answer in the register after the addition represents the total gross pay of the employee.

Computation on first employee

The figure in Address 1201, 0000003000 (3000 or assumed $30.00) is added to the figure in the register, 0000020000 (20000 or assumed $200.00) for the gross pay of 0000023000 (23000 or assumed $230.00).

Instruction number	Instruction location	Operation abbreviation	Operation code	Data address	Instruction address	Translation
20	0419	SUB	11	0703	0420	Subtract

Both Instruction 12 and 19 would yield the employee's gross pay from which the deductions must be subtracted to arrive at a net or "take-home" pay; therefore, the following instruction will be executed no matter whether any overtime pay was figured. This instruction informs the arithmetic unit to subtract the amount of Federal income tax withheld and stored in Address 0703 from the employee's gross pay now in the register. The control unit then calls for the next instruction.

Computation on first employee

The amount of Federal income tax withheld, 0000002600 (2600 or assumed $26.00) as stored in Address 0703 will be subtracted from the gross pay being held in the register 0000023000 (23000 or assumed $230.00) for an answer of 0000020400 (20400 or assumed $204.00).

Instruction number	Instruction location	Operation abbreviation	Operation code	Data address	Instruction address	Translation
21	0420	SUB	11	0704	0421	Subtract

The other deductions for the employee have been totaled and stored in Address 0704. When this total "other deduction figure" is brought into the arithmetic unit and subtracted from the figure in the register, the resulting answer will be the employee's net or take-home pay. The control unit will then call for the instruction in Address 0421.

Computation on first employee

The total other deduction amount, 0000000950 (950 or assumed $9.50) stored in Address 0704 will be subtracted from the amount in the register, 0000020400 (20400 or assumed $204.00) with resulting net pay of 0000019450 (19450 or assumed $194.50).

Instruction number	Instruction location	Operation abbreviation	Operation code	Data address	Instruction address	Translation
22	0423	HLT	09	0000	0000	

The contents of storage Address 1201 are erased and the net pay figure which was in the register is then stored in Address 1201. The control unit they analyzes the next instruction in Address 0421.

Computation on first employee

The figure 0000003000 (3000 or assumed $30.00) which was previously stored in Address 1201 is erased, the address is set to 0000000000 (0), and the net pay figure of 0000019450 (19450 or assumed $194.50) is placed in storage at 1201.

Instruction number	Instruction location	Operation abbreviation	Operation code	Data address	Instruction address	Translation
23	0422	PCH	02	1200	0401	Punch

The data placed in storage will be punched into a card beginning with data in Address 1200 and continuing through Address 1207 (the eight words capable of representation on one punched card). Data has been stored only in Addresses 1200 (employee identification number) and 1201 (net pay); so only two words will be punched per card. The next instruction will come from Address 0401 to begin processing the net pay of the next employee.

Computation on first employee

A punched card will be produced containing the employee's number 0000000008 (8) in the first word (10 columns) and his net pay 0000019450 (19450 or assumed $194.50) in the second word (Columns 11–20). The card will be stored in the hopper for printout at a later time.

Instruction number	Instruction location	Operation abbreviation	Operation code	Data address	Instruction address	Translation
24	0421	STR	06	1201	0422	Store

When the control unit interprets this code (09) as a result of the branch operation in Instruction 5, the processing of the program will be stopped. Because no additional processing is to be done, no data or instruction address will be used.

The processing of the payroll has been terminated.

Now that we have become acquainted with a simple, make-believe electronic computer, let's look at some applications requiring the services of true computers. As we discovered during our review of computer operations, two factors exclusive of equipment must be carefully planned: the stored program which will direct the processing of data, and the data taken from source documents to be fed to the computer for processing. We have seen how punched cards were used to feed in payroll data to be processed on IMCOM, and we have become acquainted with punched tape as a common language for automatic typewriters. Now let's look at some other input media.

MICR—MAGNETIC INK CHARACTER RECOGNITION

Introduction

MICR (Magnetic Ink Character Recognition) is actually another common-language medium and might have been included in the chapter on IDP. Since application of MICR systems almost always includes some computer operations the discussion of MICR has been postponed to this chapter on EDP.

Magnetic ink encoding is a process whereby specially designed numbers and symbols containing elements capable of being magnetized are printed on paper. When these magnetic characters on source documents are read, the documents are sorted and processed by highspeed electronic equipment. But the characters must be of a special type. The MICR language consists of fourteen characters, ten digits (0–9) and four special symbols. These special characters, as shown in the illustration, conform to the specifications of the ABA (American Bankers Association) in terms of type style and size. Although the mechanical process used to read the characters is very complicated, the configurations are interpreted by the readers in terms of the number of magnetic bits contained in a character and the location of those bits.

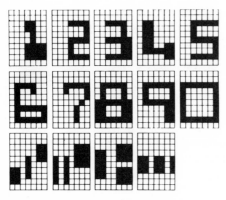

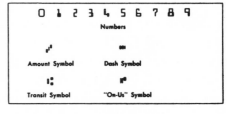

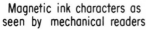

Magnetic ink characters as seen by mechanical readers

Magnetic ink characters as seen by human eyes

Magnetic ink used to record the characters is a printers' ink which contains ground iron oxide particles that can serve as electrical conductors. The ink thus can produce a character that can be temporarily magnetized to create a magnetic field when subjected to an electric charge. The name "magnetic ink" is somewhat misleading in that the ink is not magnetized until the inked characters are passed under a device which then charges them. Immediately after being magnetized, each character containing the magnetized bits is passed under a reading device which interprets the specific character. Each time the characters are to be read they are remagnetized immediately before the scanning of the encoded document.

The characters are commonly pre-encoded on documents by offset machines. Variable information may be typed on later by using special typewriter ribbons containing inks with iron oxide particles. But it is important that the imprinting of data be of the highest quality because processing accuracy is dependent upon the quality of the printing. Special type face must be used to encode MICR characters as printed characters (see p. 194). This style of print was developed to meet the MICR qualifications as well as to be meaningful to human reading.

MICR Application—Banking

MICR has its major application in banking operations. Because the MICR processing system depends upon the use of magnetically encoded checks, all depositors of the specific banks are supplied with personalized imprinted checks and deposit slips free of charge. Although a depositor's name and address may be printed on the check, usually in the upper left corner, the only significant printing required to process the check electronically is printed on one line with magnetic ink and placed at the bottom of the check. The printing is so laid out that the last MICR number encoded will appear approximately ¼ inch from the right edge of the check, and the entire line will be approximately ⅜ inch from the bottom edge. The overall size of the check is unimportant and may vary in commercial and personal checks; but, in respect to the right and bottom edges, the placement of the coding must be the same on all checks.

As shown in the check illustration, the first group of encoded numbers, the routing symbol and the transit number, contains digits needed to identify the depositor's bank. The numbers also appear at the upper right of the check in regular printing style. Approximately fifty years ago the ABA developed a plan for numbering all banks in the country so that each would have an identifying number. In the example shown, the digits indicate that the

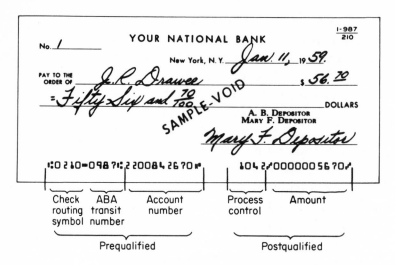

check was written on bank number 987 which is located in New York City (identified by the number 1); the 210 identifies the Federal Reserve district and branch.

$$\text{Number identifying New York City area} \rightarrow \frac{1\text{-}987}{210} \leftarrow \text{ABA number identifying individual bank on a nationwide basis}$$

Federal Reserve routing number which identifies the Federal Reserve district and the Federal Reserve branch bank number

Like the first field just discussed (the transit field), the second field (the account number field) is also prequalified. Checks are MICR encoded with the constant data before being distributed to the account holder for his use. The account number field contains the following information:

1. The number of the branch bank in which the depositor has established his checking account.

2. A check digit which permits the computer to verify the accuracy of its reading operation.

3. The account number assigned to the depositor.

Processing of the outstanding checks will be done by the depositor's account number, not by his name. As noted earlier (p. 74), data processing requiring a large amount of input data is usually done by code numbers rather than by alphabetic letters. Because it is very important that the amount of a written check be deducted from the balance of the correct checking account, a digit called a *check digit* is inserted in the depositor's account number. We need not concern ourselves with the placement of the check digit or how it actually works to verify a number; that is meaningful only to the computer. In the account number of 842670 shown on the illustrated check, we do not know which digit in this number serves as the check digit. The programmers must tell the computer exactly where the check digit is located and how it is to be used to verify the other digits, but the check digit has no significance to the writer of the check or to those handling the check. The remaining part of the account number (the digits "22" shown in the illustration) represents the number of the branch operated by Your National Bank.

As previously mentioned, these two fields, the transit field and the account field, are pre-encoded before the blanks are distributed to the depositor for his writing of checks. The remaining MICR codes are placed on the check after the check has been written and is presented for payment.

BRANCH BANK OPERATION. When the written check is presented to a bank for payment, the remaining two items, the process control (transaction) number and the amount of the check, are encoded on the check. This encoding of the last two fields is done at the bank when the checks are being processed on a "proof" machine on which the operator lists the checks individually and then sorts each encoded check into special pockets allocated for "on us" checks (checks written by the depositor on the bank processing the checks), out-of-state checks, government checks, and other special categories. After the check is placed in the proof or encoder machine, the amount of the check is keyed into the keyboard along with the process control code. When the operator depresses the activation bar, the amount and the control code are printed at the bottom of the check; and the same figures are recorded on a listing tape to be used for later processing. The operator then removes the check and places the encoded check in the proper sorting pocket where it becomes one item in a "batch" of items.

Different banking organizations use different process control codes to designate the type of transactions the document represents. Because most checks represent an instruction by the depositor to deduct the written amount from the account balance, some banks omit encoding such a transaction; when the computer finds nothing in this location of the check to read, it knows from previous instructions that the document represents such a transaction. Many exceptions may occur, however; and each operation which enlarges, restricts, or changes the original instruction requires a different process control code. As many as 100 different transactions may be assigned code numbers for this field.

The fourth and last field appearing on the check represents the amount for which the check was written. Ten digits are always used for this field with zeros filling unused spaces to the left of the actual amount. Decimals and dollar signs are omitted. Because the check illustrated (p. 196) was written for $56.70, the 10-digit amount encoded at the bottom appears as 0000005670.

Although we have discussed the content of the four fields, we have not mentioned the peculiar little marks encoded with the digits. These small characters (see p. 194) are called *cue characters*; they represent no numerical data but merely serve to separate the fields. (For further discussion see p. 200.)

COMPUTER OPERATIONS. After the checks have been processed at the branch banks and the four fields are complete, the checks are sent in batches to the centralized processing installation. In large banking organizations, one check-processing computer with its supporting equipment will process all checks and other documents received from many branch banks located in the metropolitan area and in nearby localities. Every work-day evening, messengers collect the documents from the branch banks and take them to the computer center. Each branch will have batched the various types of documents into batches of 150, and the total per batch is rechecked at the computer center. Clerks then fan through the batches to check that all staples and paper clips have been removed and that all documents are face up with the bottom edge down. Batch cards are placed in front of each batch to facilitate sorting and finding documents in the event of errors. The jogger, a vibrating machine, then receives the batches and jogs them into position so all documents are even on the bottom and right edge.

The stacked documents are placed in the feed hopper of the sorter which reads the encoded numbers and cue characters at the bottom of each document. As the documents go through the sorter one at a time, the iron oxide in the encoded characters is mag-

MICR sorter/reader.

netized just before the documents pass under the read-head of the sorter. The read-head analyzes the placement and amount of metal particles in each character capable of sending out an electric impulse; each character (p. 194) sends out a different design of impulses. After the sorter picks up these impulses, the information is transmitted directly to the computer which receives the information, makes approximately 800 decisions, and returns a message to the sorter telling it which of 13 available sorting pockets is to receive the document.

The computer not only directs the sorter to place the check in the proper sorter pocket, it also captures all the encoded data from the check when the check passes the reading mechanism. This encoded data is placed in the computer's storage facilities for future processing. It will not be necessary for the computer to obtain any additional data from the check at any future time. Once the data from the check is captured and placed in storage within the computer, it can be recalled whenever the records and reports needed are to be processed. Thus one pass of the check provides the means for sorting the check and for updating all future records affected by the written check.

As noted before, the sizes of documents to be processed may vary considerably; therefore, it is important that the coding be placed in fields identically located at the bottom and right edge of each document. As the document leaves the stack to be read, the right edge leads the way; and the fields are read from right to left, with the unit value being read first, then the tens, the hundreds, the thousands, etc.

To facilitate reading the digits, the designers of the system created cue characters to tell the computer where certain data begins and where it ends. Note the sample check (p. 196) and the cue characters (p. 194). As the check leaves the batch and starts through the sorter, the first character to be read at the right is the cue character ▄▎■ , the amount symbol that tells the computer to accept the following digits as the amount or value on the face of the document. After ten digits have been read and interpreted, the same symbol is repeated to tell the computer that the amount is completed and a new field, the process control field, is next in line. The next cue character ▐▐■ , the "on-us" symbol which instructs the computer that the document is one belonging to a depositor in this banking organization, is read; and the data is sent to the computer for checking and processing. The fourth cue character ▐▄ , the transit symbol, tells the computer that the following digits pertain to the location of the bank upon which the check is drawn. The transit number is separated by a dash cue character ■ ■ ▐ to permit the computer to differentiate the transit number from the routing symbol.

The documents are processed so rapidly through the sorter that the human eye is unable to see any specific documents but sees only a continuous, blurred line of paper. Although it is impossible to describe the operating speed of the sorter and the computer in a meaningful way, some of the specifications are interesting.

The encoded characters on the documents may be read at the rate of 30,000 characters per second—snap your fingers and 30,000 digits and cue characters have passed on to the computer.

Approximately 1,560 documents can be read, interpreted, and placed in specific pockets for each minute, 26 documents per second.

Each time a document is read and the data sent to the computer, the computer performs approximately 800 calculations and then returns a message to the sorter telling it where to pocket the document—800 decisions in 1/26 second. The document moved less than 8 inches from the time the characters were read to the time the computer returned its message.

Thus we have seen how the source document containing the data encoded in ink capable of being magnetized can supply the necessary data for computer processing. After the computer receives the data, a great deal of processing must be done before the finished reports are available. Data must be classified, daily transactions recorded, and various files on magnetic tape updated so that the computer can furnish data to the printers to produce the following reports:

1. Status report containing the account number, correct balance, and date of last activity for each account

2. Rejected items register listing all documents not accepted by the computer

3. Journal reflecting all transaction details

4. Overdrawn accounts report

5. Report of accounts that have been reduced to a zero balance during the day's posting.

We have seen how bank documents can be electronically processed through use of magnetic ink. Other than encoding the amount and the process control in branch banks, human handling has been almost eliminated and processing accuracy and speed greatly increased. MICR, brought on by banks' need to keep pace with the snowballing burden of paperwork, has revolutionized bank accounting.

OPTICAL READERS

Introduction

Modern computers can perform thousands of calculations per second, but we must recognize one major shortcoming which restricts the full utilization of this tremendous speed. This shortcoming, sometimes referred to as the "missing link" in data processing, is the relatively slow means of input. Computers are being built to calculate faster; magnetic tapes are being designed to contain more data and to read faster; printers are being made that can print much faster—yet the main source of data input remains linked to punched cards. And card punching continues at the same rate of punching. Because most computers cannot read documents designed for human interpretation, coding information for computers is slow, expensive, and inaccurate. To overcome this major barrier, more than twenty companies are developing optical readers, machines that can scan words, numbers, symbols, and special marks, and translate the scanned characters directly into a compatible machine language.

As noted in discussing MICR, characters imprinted with ink bits capable of being magnetized provide character readers with input data. Optical readers, however, operate on an entirely different principle and have no relationship to MICR characters or reading methods. It is not practical in this book to describe the highly technical operations of optical readers. Various companies manufacturing optical readers have developed different reading methods. All methods are extremely complicated. As with computer circuitry, it is not necessary to understand how those methods work in order to appreciate the usefulness of the media.

Optical reading is similar to human reading. When we look at a printed paper, we see the images of letters, numbers, pictures, etc. These images are transmitted back to the brain which, because of previous learning, recognizes the images and classifies them into specific meanings. Optical scanning equipment also views a paper, converts the images, or what it "sees," into electric energy and deciphers the images it recognizes according to the logic or memory built into it. Of course, characters for the scanner to read must all rigidly conform to predetermined formats and cannot vary in size and shape. Persons can recognize varying and distorted characters; optical scanners cannot. People read by seeing an entire image at a glance; optical scanners analyze only a tiny portion of an image at a time and then combine the portions in order to interpret the entire image. Even by applying numerous analyses to each image, the optical scanner reads much faster than a person, but since its "intelligence" is limited, it can recognize only certain types of images. Basically, the reading operations follow a powerful beam of light flashed on the reading area. Black and white patterns of reflected light are detected, and those patterns are converted into electronic impulses identifying the characters read.

Most data processing systems using optical scanners for providing input data are *on-line* readers, readers under the control of the computer and providing data directly to the computer. The need to encode source data into punched cards, punched tape, or magnetic tape for entry into a computer is eliminated by optical scanning because the original business document is as meaningful to processing machines as it is to human readers.

Some optical readers are capable of electronically reading 1,500 characters per second (much faster than the human eye can read) and handling as many as 400 documents per minute. Up to 1,500 documents may be placed in the feed hopper at one time to assure continuous reading operations. But optical readers are selective. Some can read documents of a certain weight of white paper only. Others cannot function with different shades of ink or smudges, paper folds, or perforations. And they cannot read any and all types and styles of characters or marks; specific makes of readers can read only specially designed letters, numbers, or symbols. For example, the IBM 1428 Reader can read only 42 different characters (upper case letters A through Z, numbers 0 through 9, and some commonly used symbols).

The Reader's Digest Club made in 1955 one of the earliest applications of optical scanning. The club was mailing over 20,000,000 books each year and was forced to recruit temporary help to handle this heavy mail load. To eliminate some of the human inefficiencies in the system, the company purchased a reading machine from Intelligent Machines Research, a small firm now known as Farrington Manufacturing Company, one of the nation's leading producers of optical reading machines. The Digest officials reported that the optical reader saved its original purchase price every six months by reducing labor costs and increasing efficiency.

Code Readers

PRINCIPLE OF OPERATION. The Addressograph-Multigraph Corporation has developed an optical code to be used on its readers which electronically read the coded data imprinted on documents. The code, as may be noted in the illustration on p. 204, consists of vertical dashes. The number code allocates two short dashes or one long dash for each number, and various numbers are

```
┌─────────────────────────┐
│  I 23  456  789  0       │
│  ▪▪    ▪     ▮ ▪▪  ▮     │
│  ▪ ▪▪  ▪▪ ▮    ▪ ▪▪      │
└─────────────────────────┘
```

designated by the positioning of the short or long dashes. As previously noted, the dashes do not contain iron oxide used in MICR operations but are interpreted by the optical scanner by the placement and type of dashes appearing on the document.

Plastic identification plates are made on a Graphotype machine similar to that illustrated on p. 00. Most embossed plates contain the person's name, his identification number, and the dash code representing the identification number.

When the owner of the ID plastic plate presents his plate at the scene of the transaction, the embossed plate is laid in a data recorder machine and a tabulating card containing at least one carbon copy is placed on top of the ID plate. The information on the plate will be transferred to the tabulating card as the clerk rolls a pressure roller over the plate and the card. All the data on the embossed card is constant; if the ID number should ever change, a new plate would have to be made. If a plate is used in an operation where variable data is also recorded on the tabulating card, recording machines may be used that contain numeric lever settings. When the sale is made, the sales clerk moves the numeric levers to the desired settings. As the print roller moves across the tab card, the constant data from the ID plate is recorded on one end of the tab card; the variable data from the numeric settings is recorded on the other end. Thus a written document at the point of the transaction has been created. The ID plate and the carbon copy is given to the customer; the original is stacked with other tab cards for future processing.

The stacked tab cards are later gathered and fed to the optical code reader which scans the dashes or bar code imprinted on each card and punches the cards with the Hollerith code, the code used by most card processing machines. Actually, the reading operation results in the translation of the bar code into the Hollerith code and changes the sales card from a tab card to a punched card. The punched card can now serve as input for a wide variety of computers.

The unpunched card (3) in the illustration on p. 206 is the

d as it comes off the stack of sales cards. After the card has
n fed to the reader and the bar code has been interpreted, the
der punches the translated data into the same card, as shown at
right in the illustration, (4).

This type of operation is an *off-line* operation because data is not
ectly fed to the computer but is first translated into an acceptable
chine language. Why not use punched cards to begin with?
eating punched cards in such a business transaction would require
uman operation for punching in the data; and this is the type
operation we are trying to avoid in order to decrease costs and to
rease accuracy. No manual key-punching is needed when optical
le readers are used. Thus, such a system has two obvious ad-
tages:

1. Manual key-punching is eliminated by automatically processing recorded data for use as input in other EDP machines.

2. Accurate input is assured, and erroneous punching of source
documents is eliminated.

OPTICAL CODE READER APPLICATION. A business
eration using the optical code with a tab card and punched
d is illustrated on p. 206. The embossed plastic card con-
ing the name of the owner, his identification number, and
bar code representing the ID number is the principal factor in
application. The card is inserted in the illustrated recorder.
e illustration assumes that the variable data of 12345 ($123.45) is
be recorded on the tab card. To record this amount, the numeric
ers on the recorder are moved to the proper settings. As the
ler below the black handle is moved across the tab card that was
erted on top of the plastic ID plate, the tab card is produced con-
ning the bar codes for the constant ID data to the left and the
iable data to the right. After the tab card has been fed to the
tical reader and the code has been interpreted, the data repre-
ted by the recorded bar codes is translated into the Hollerith
le and punched into the tab card. The original tab card made
the point of sale can now serve as input to a computer to tell the
nputer that the person by the name of 123 456 789 0 made a
rchase of $123.45.

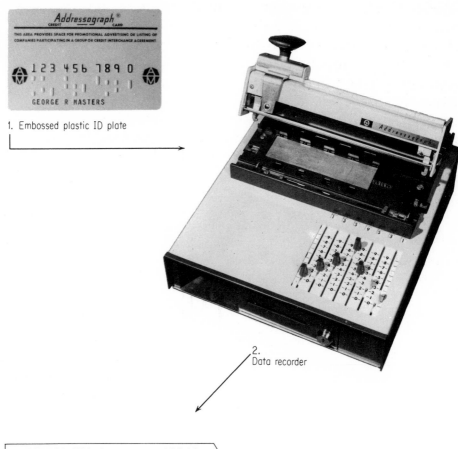

1. Embossed plastic ID plate

2. Data recorder

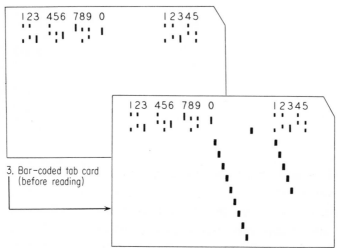

3. Bar-coded tab card (before reading)

4. Punched tab card (after reading)

Optical code reader application.

Character Readers

The character reader is more complex than the optical code
reader because it is not restricted to recognizing a standardized bar
code but can scan and interpret letters, numbers, and symbols; no
coding of data, such as bar codes, is necessary. Characters read by
human eyes can be read by the scanner's "eyes." Because of the
many variable factors involved in reading direct copy, most scanners
can read only one predesigned letter and numeric style. One of the
most common character fonts was developed by the National Cash
Register Company. Notice some peculiarities in the number designs
shown in the illustration.

```
0                    10.00 8 |
1 1 1 1 1 1 1 1.1 1 8 |
2 2 2 2 2 2 2 2.2 2 8 |
3 3 3 3 3 3 3 3.3 3 8 |
4 4 4 4 4 4 4 4.4 4 8 |
5 5 5 5 5 5 5 5.5 5 8 |
6 6 6 6 6 6 6 6.6 6 8 |
7 7 7 7 7 7 7 7.7 7 8 |
8 8 8 8 8 8 8 8.8 8 8 |
9 9 9 9 9 9 9 9.9 9 8 |
0
0                     .0 0 1 |
0
0                     .0 0 6 |
0
0                     .0 0 4 |
0                     .0 0 0 |
```

Much more sophisticated optical readers are being developed.
One large company has already demonstrated a reader that scanned
the pages of a Russian book and translated the Russian language
into English. Even reading and interpreting handwriting may not
be far away. At present, using these complex readers is extremely
costly; where simplified character fonts are used, however, large-
scale operations are economically feasible.

Character code for optical readers.

Oil companies use one of the most common applications
optical character readers. Because the operation is similar to t
previously cited in describing the reading of codes, another detai
description is unnecessary. The two operations differ in that
needs an intermediary bar code for interpretation and the otl
needs only the printed letter, number, or symbol.

After the sale has been recorded on the sales slip as previou
described, the original sales slip containing the amount of the p
chase and the customer's identification number is sent to the
company's data processing center where, along with sales slips fr
all its outlets, the sales slips will be optically read and the data
to the computer. Constant data, such as the date of sale, applica
to all charges for a day's operation may not be optically read
fed to the computer only once in the form of a program card.
in MICR processing of checks, the data read is used to update
files stored within the computer. Instead of producing a ba
statement as the MICR operation does, the computer periodica
relays its filed information to a high-speed printer which produ
statements for each charge customer. As a result, the input data
made available without any handwritten entries at the point
sale. And the constant data embossed on the credit card is accura
the only chance for error is the manual setting of the amount lev
on the recording machine.

This type of operation, providing input directly from sales sli

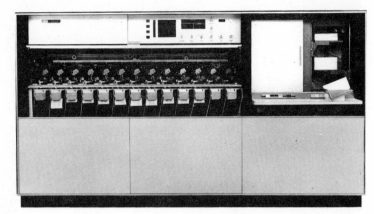

Courtesy of the IBM Corporation.

tical character reader.

becoming increasingly popular in today's business world. Data
ocessing costs are reduced by eliminating tedious manual book-
eping tasks; further, accurate records can be produced more rap-
y, and managerial control is more efficient as a result of central-
d record processing.

VIEW QUESTIONS

True–False

1. Data placed in computer storage may be either constant data or
   variable data.

2. Most business problems processed on a computer contain some
   branching and looping instructions.

3. When a "read" command is executed, the data contained in the
   storage address into which new data is to be placed is automatically lost.

4. Decimal numbers must always contain a decimal point when fed
   to IMCOM and require one storage cell per decimal just as one
   digit requires one storage cell.

5. The various sections or "syllables" in IMCOM's instructions
   must always designate similar categories of operations—the data
   address must be used for data addresses only.

6. All computers are manufactured with odd-parity checks.

7. All banks use the same style of numbers and symbols when us
a MICR system.

8. Basically, optical scanners are capable of reading a document
interpreting the reflected light.

9. A more sophisticated reader is needed in optical character re
ing than in optical code reading.

10. All character readers must use the same standardized font.

Multiple Choice

1. A key word used to describe EDP applications is

    a. Computer
    b. Punched cards
    c. Optical scanner
    d. IMCOM.

2. A computer's storage address may contain

    a. Data
    b. Instructions
    c. Data and instructions
    d. Data, instructions, and punched cards.

3. Branching operations result from comparisons of values wh
may be

    a. Only one value
    b. One of two values
    c. One of three values
    d. One of four values.

4. The purpose of a block diagram is to

    a. Place each needed program instruction in a block or graph
    b. Show only those program sections requiring branching a
    looping operations.
    c. Use universally accepted blocks to describe graphically
    operations.
    d. Graphically describe the logic and sequences of needed ope
    tions to be later coded into instructions.

5. The first card to be fed to a computer, such as IMCOM, wou
be a

    a. Housekeeping card
    b. Call for instruction card

c. Instruction card
d. Data card.

6. The essential component of a computer because it supplies the instructions and data for each processing step is the

a. Input unit
b. Storage unit
c. Control unit
d. Arithmetic unit.

7. The system which is not truly an optical scanning system is the

a. Character reader
b. Code reader
c. Plastic card embossed code reader
d. MICR and reader.

8. Checks of various sizes can be read on a check reader or sorter because

a. The number and character code is the same on all checks.
b. All data is similarly located near the right edge and bottom of checks.
c. Prelistings are made before checks are sorted.
d. Numbers and characters are magnetized at all times to give off electric impulses.

9. Currently, the greatest obstacle to rapid data processing in large programs is

a. Slow input
b. Slow storage
c. Limited storage capacity
d. Difficulty in writing programs.

0. The major problem in accuracy of input data in optical reading systems is the result of

a. Human error problems in recording sales amounts
b. Improper reading of printed characters by scanners
c. Excessive speed in scanning devices
d. Limitations on managerial control.

Discussion

. What three kinds of data does an IMCOM instruction contain?

. Why is the analogy of computer storage addresses to post office boxes contradictory?

. Why is it necessary to have housekeeping operations in a program?

4. What are the advantages and disadvantages of core storage?

5. What five units make up the necessary components in all cc puters and what functions do they perform?

6. What are the various types of direct reading systems and wl types of businesses would be likely to use them?

Vocabulary

Define the following terms in your own words:

Address	Diagramming	Register
Storage	Coding	Arithmetic unit
Instruction	Stored program	Hard copy
Branching	Housekeeping card	MICR
Looping	Cell	Cue character
Variable data	Odd parity	Code reader
Constant data	Core	Character reader
Block diagram	Plane	Character font
Counter	Control unit	

Computer Problems

Section I—Supplying Results

Operation Codes	Storage Addresses — Stored Values

03	Shift to the right	1000 — 4
04	Shift to the left	1001 — 6
05	Reset and load the register	1002 — 20
06	Store in specified location	1003 — 2
08	Branch on positive	1004 — 10
09	Halt	1500 — 0 (for storage)
10	Add	
11	Subtract	
12	Multiply	
13	Divide	

Use the foregoing operation codes and stored values to find the n merical values (answers) to the following problems. The 10-digit i structions as given in the IMCOM illustration will be used for t following problems:

X X	X X X X	X X X X
Oper- ation Code	Data Address	Next In- struction Address

EXAMPLE

Instruction

Address	Instruction		Result
0001	05 1000 0002	=	4 (set register to 0; insert 4)
0002	10 1002 0003	=	4 + 20 or 24
0003	13 1001 0004	=	24 + 6 or 4
0004	09 0000 0000	=	answer of 4

Problem 1

Instruction

Address	Instruction		Result
0001	05 1002 0002	=	
0002	12 1000 0003	=	
0003	13 1004 0004	=	
0004	12 1003 0005	=	
0005	13 1000 0006	=	
0006	09 0000 0000	=	

Problem 2

Instruction

Address	Instruction		Result
0001	05 1001 0002	=	
0002	10 1002 0003	=	
0003	10 1004 0004	=	
0004	13 1001 0005	=	
0005	11 1003 0006	=	
0006	12 1004 0007	=	
0007	13 1002 0008	=	
0008	09 0000 0000	=	

Problem 3

Instruction

Address	Instruction		Result
0001	05 1004 0002	=	
0002	12 1002 0003	=	
0003	13 1000 0004	=	

0004	03 0001 0005	=
0005	12 1001 0006	=
0006	11 1004 0007	=
0007	09 0000 0000	=

Problem 4

Instruction Address	Instruction		Result
0001	05 1003 0002	=	
0002	04 0002 0003	=	
0003	13 1002 0004	=	
0004	10 1001 0005	=	
0005	13 1000 0006	=	
0006	09 0000 0000	=	

Problem 5

Instruction Address	Instruction		Result
0001	05 1000 0002	=	
0002	04 0001 0003	=	
0003	06 1500 0004	=	
0004	11 1002 0005	=	
0005	08 0008 0006	=	
0006	05 1002 0007	=	
0007	12 1003 0010	=	
0008	05 1500 0009	=	
0009	13 1004 0010	=	
0010	09 0000 0000	=	

Section II — Supplying Instruction Codes

Supply the necessary 10-digit instruction code needed to provide the calculation given under "Result." Use the operation codes, storage addresses, and stored values given on p. 212.

EXAMPLE

Instruction Address	Instruction	Result
0001	05 1002 0002	Set register to 0; insert value of 20.
0002	13 1000 0003	Divide 4 into 20 to get value of 5.
0003	12 1003 0004	Multiply 5 by 2 to get product of 10.
0004	09 0000 0000	Halt processing operations.

Problem 1

Instruction Address	Instruction	Result
0001	— ____ ____	Set register to 0; insert value of 10.
0002	— ____ ____	Add 4 to 10 to get sum of 14.
0003	— ____ ____	Subtract 2 from 14 to get remainder of 12.
0004	— ____ ____	Divide 6 into 12 to get quotient of 2.
0005	— ____ ____	Halt processing operations.

Problem 2

Instruction Address	Instruction	Result
0001	— ____ ____	Set register to 0; insert value of 4.
0002	— ____ ____	Divide 2 into 4 to get quotient of 2.
0003	— ____ ____	Add 20 to 2 to get sum of 22.
0004	— ____ ____	Add 2 to 22 to get sum of 24.
0005	— ____ ____	Divide 6 into 24 to get quotient of 4.
0006	— ____ ____	Multiply 4 by 10 to get product of 40.
0007	— ____ ____	Subtract 2 from 40 to get remainder of 38.
0008	— ____ ____	Halt processing operations.

Problem 3

Instruction Address	Instruction	Result
0001	— ____ ____	Set register to 0; insert value of 6.
0002	— ____ ____	Multiply 6 by 10 to get product of 60.
0003	— ____ ____	Subtract 10 from 60 to get remainder of 50.
0004	— ____ ____	Shift 1 place to right to get value of 5.
0005	— ____ ____	Multiply 5 by 2 to get product of 10.
0006	— ____ ____	Add 4 to 10 to get sum of 14.
0007	— ____ ____	Halt processing operations.

Problem 4

Instruction Address	Instruction	Result
0001	— ____ ____	Reset register to 0; insert value of 4.
0002	— ____ ____	Subtract 2 from 4 to get remainder of 2.
0003	— ____ ____	Shift left 2 places to get value of 200.
0004	— ____ ____	Divide 20 into 200 to get quotient of 10.
0005	— ____ ____	Add 6 to 10 to get sum of 16.
0006	— ____ ____	Halt processing operations.

Problem 5

Instruction Address	Instruction	Result
0001	__ ____ ____	Reset register to 0; insert value of 6.
0002	__ ____ ____	Shift left 2 places to get value of 600.
0003	__ ____ ____	Divide 20 into 600 to get quotient of 30.
0004	__ ____ ____	Store value of 30 in Address 1500 for later use.
0005	__ ____ ____	Subtract 10 from 30 to get remainder of 20.
0006	__ ____ ____	Branch to Instruction 0009 if value in register is positive; go to 0007 if negative.
0007	__ ____ ____	Divide 10 into 20 to get quotient of 2.
0008	__ ____ ____	Add 4 to 2 to get sum of 6.
0009	__ ____ ____	Reset register to 0; insert value of 30.
0010	__ ____ ____	Divide 10 into 30 to get quotient of 3.
0011	__ ____ ____	Halt processing operations.

Section III — Supplying Instruction Codes and Results

Supply the necessary instruction address, instruction code, and result comments to achieve the answer requested in the problem. Use the operation codes, storage addresses, and stored values given in the chart on p. 212.

EXAMPLE

Use 3 instructions to obtain a value of 26 and halt processing operations.

Instruction Address	Instruction	Result
0001	05 1002 0002	Reset register to 0; insert value of 20.
0002	10 1001 0003	Add 6 to 20 to get sum of 26.
0003	09 0000 0000	Halt processing operations.

Problem 1. Use 3 instructions to obtain a value of 22 and halt processing operations.

Instruction Address	Instruction	Result
____	__ ____ ____	_____
____	__ ____ ____	_____
____	__ ____ ____	_____

Problem 2. Use 4 instructions to obtain a value of 62 and halt processing operations.

Instruction
Address   *Instruction*   *Result*

_____   __ ____ ____   _____
_____   __ ____ ____   _____
_____   __ ____ ____   _____
_____   __ ____ ____   _____
_____   __ ____ ____   _____

Problem 3. Use 4 instructions to obtain a value of 78 and halt processing operations.

Instruction
Address   *Instruction*   *Result*

_____   __ ____ ____   _____
_____   __ ____ ____   _____
_____   __ ____ ____   _____
_____   __ ____ ____   _____

Problem 4. Use 4 instructions to obtain a value of 7 and halt processing operations.

Instruction
Address   *Instruction*   *Result*

_____   __ ____ ____   _____
_____   __ ____ ____   _____
_____   __ ____ ____   _____
_____   __ ____ ____   _____

Problem 5. Use 7 instructions to obtain a value of 4003 and halt
processing operations.

Instruction
Address   *Instruction*   *Result*

_____   __ ____ ____   _____
_____   __ ____ ____   _____
_____   __ ____ ____   _____
_____   __ ____ ____   _____
_____   __ ____ ____   _____
_____   __ ____ ____   _____
_____   __ ____ ____   _____

Example of

PROGRAMMING APTITUDE TEST

Part I

The six numbers to the left follow a specific sequence. Select one of the numbers at the right that continues the series. (Time: 3 minutes)

Example:

						(a)	(b)	(c)	(d)	(e)
2	4	6	8	10	12	10	12	14	16	18

In the preceding example, the answer is (c) because it continues the sequence of adding 2 to the previous number.

							(a)	(b)	(c)	(d)	(e)
(1)	9	12	15	18	21	24	23	25	26	27	28
(2)	44	37	30	23	16	9	1	2	3	4	5
(3)	21	22	24	27	31	36	38	39	40	41	42
(4)	12	11	9	8	6	5	1	2	3	4	5
(5)	26	23	26	24	26	25	23	24	25	26	27
(6)	3	2	1	3	2	1	1	2	3	4	5
(7)	4	7	14	17	34	37	40	44	51	71	74
(8)	54	18	36	12	24	8	2	6	12	16	20
(9)	21	24	28	23	17	24	19	22	25	28	32
(10)	4	6	18	8	10	30	18	20	24	26	28

Part II

In the three figures to the left, Fig. 1 has a specific relationship to Fig. 2. Select one of the figures at the right that has a similar relationship to Fig. 3. (*Time:* 3 minutes)

Example:

In the foregoing example, the answer is Fig. b because it is the inverted form of Fig. 3 as Fig. 2 is the inverted form of Fig. 1.

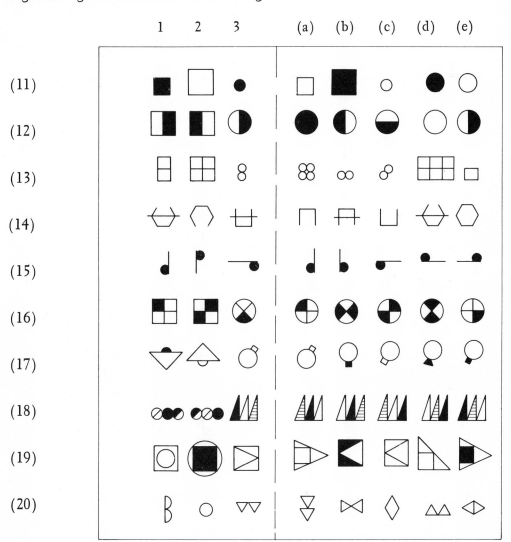

Part III

Select one of the numbers given below each problem as the correct answer to the problem. Time: 3 minutes)

Example:

How many pencils can you buy with 20 cents when the pencils sell for 48 cents a dozen?

(a) 2 (b) 3 (c) 4 (d) 5 (e) 6

In the preceding example, the answer is (d) because each pencil costs 4 cents.

21. If after six weeks you have saved $22.50, how much have you averaged per week in your savings?

(a) $3.50 (b) $3.75 (c) $2.75 (d) $4.25 (e) $4.50

22. The width of an envelope is 3¼ inches. If the envelope is a total of 39 square inches, how long is the envelope?

(a) 11½ in. (b) 12 in. (c) 12½ in. (d) 8½ in. (e) 6 in.

23. A punched-card sorter can sort 350 cards per minute. If 1,400 cards must be run through the sorter three times, how many minutes will be needed to complete the sorting?

(a) 54 min (b) 52 min (c) 24 min (d)) 12 min (e) 8 min

24. For what amount would you write a check for six ball-point pens at 40 cents each and four fountain pens at $6 per dozen?

(a) $3.20 (b) $5.40 (c) $6.20 (d) $2.20 (e) $4.40

25. If there are 4 sophomores, 12 juniors, and 36 seniors in a data processing class and the class is expanded with similar proportions until enrollment reaches 78, how many juniors will be in the class?

(a) 14 (b) 15 (c) 16 (d) 18 (e) 22

AUTOMATED DATA PROCESSING
PERSONNEL PROBLEMS

INTRODUCTION

Many books, pamphlets, and articles have been written on the sociological and economic problems resulting from the prevailing automation revolution. Labor leaders, public officials, business managers, economists—all have expressed pleasure, concern, or sorrow at the introduction of automation into American business. Electronic data processing has brought many recognized advantages and disadvantages—some, real; some, imaginary. Some problems were the cause of automation; some were the result. Fundamentally, the problems created by electronic data processing resemble those created by factory automation and mechanization, for when machines replace workers, some widespread production problems and human anxieties are bound to arise; and when problems involve the human factor, the causes of various effects are difficult to pinpoint.

Accurate and significant statistics pertaining to office automation problems are very limited in number and narrow in scope. Hence it is somewhat risky to generalize about the effects of automation. Adequate research is not available even though millions of dollars have been granted by government, business concerns, and labor unions to study the multitude of problems created by automated data processing. Even the terminology pertaining to automation processes is not standardized in meaning. As yet, there isn't even a universally accepted definition of the word "automation." As noted earlier (p. 7), something is truly automatic when it functions without a person to control it. But this rarely happens in data processing or in production. There appears to be a growing trend to label the more sophisticated mechanized operations "automation" even though such operations are not truly automated. Perhaps statistics and standardization are lacking because the automation revolution is still in its infancy and is proceding quite slowly. The shift from manual to automated procedures in offices has not occurred as rapidly as the automating of factory production lines. The continuity of office operations cannot be interrupted, and it is impossible to "stockpile" ahead as in factory production. Also, it is more difficult to install a new system in the office than in the factory because duplicate efforts are required to test new procedures. One procedure cannot be terminated until the substitute procedure has been tested and proved.

Much attention directed toward automation has been negative in tone. Automation has been the scapegoat for many individuals who simply cannot adequately explain an unsatisfactory situation. They "follow the leader" and label computers as mindless monsters that, along with their bloodless brothers, have made persons either unemployed or push-button baby sitters to these heartless creatures. Rather than follow this popular line and whirl another lash at the automation whipping boy, many freethinking individuals have suggested that other complex factors may play a role in our sociological and economic problems:

1. Inadequate demand for goods and services

2. Slow national growth rate in production

3. Poor education and training of potential employees

4. Rapid population growth, adding over a million workers a year to the labor force.

Actually, a great many jobs would be lost if companies did not recognize the importance of automation and thus try to improve their competitive positions in business.

EMPLOYMENT PROBLEMS

Some people support automation; others oppose it. The opposition refers to the unemployment problem as evidence supporting their view. They believe that although this advanced technology has created some jobs, it has eliminated far more. Of course, one can always find statistics to support a specific viewpoint. Whether these statistics are representative is a different question. Mr. Wallace Webber, president of a United Auto Workers local stated the following: "Three years ago Local 889 had 5,000 members. Now we have 4,000, and the loss mostly is due to the inroads of automation in offices." * A prominent professor of mathematics declared that this new automation revolution would "produce an unemployment situation in comparison with which . . . the depression of the 1930's will seem like a pleasant joke." †

But much evidence substantiates the assertion that employment increases as a result of technological changes. The creation of the automobile did destroy products and services associated with the horse and buggy; the invention of electricity did doom gaslights; yet, these two new inventions created undreamed of industries of huge magnitude in comparison to carriage and wagon manufacture and the making and use of illuminating gas. Since the telephone industry first started replacing its "number, please" girls with dial telephones in 1920, employment increased from 200,000 to 600,000; since 1946, employment has jumped 28 percent. There is no question that many, many jobs now exist that were unknown when electronic data processing was born about twenty years ago. Perhaps the problem we should be concerned with pertains less to the elimination of former jobs than to the creation of an adequate number of new jobs to support the growing labor force.

Even the term *unemployment* is somewhat confusing because there is a difference between an unemployed worker and a displaced worker. A displaced worker is one who is temporarily out of work as a result of job elimination; a displaced worker becomes unemployed only when he cannot find another job within a reason-

* Wallace Webber, "Office Automation Hits UAW," *Business Week*, Apr. 9, 1960, p. 58.
† Norbert Wiener, "Is Automation Really a Job Killer?" *Business Week*, Feb. 24, 1962, p. 47.

able time. The major problem resulting from automation in the office is one of transfer; it is a displacement problem rather than an unemployment problem.

Many companies have attempted to reduce displacement through intracompany transfers and through company-sponsored retraining programs. Most companies are reluctant to dismiss regular workers because company prestige suffers severely and employee morale sinks rapidly. To eliminate this negative reaction, companies have permitted normal attrition to reduce their surplus manpower and thus allow normal turnover to disguise the true problem. Even though the United States Bureau of Labor Statistics shows that a very small percentage of regular workers are laid off as a direct result of automation, the statistics are not as revealing as they appear to be. When business fluctuations are on the downturn, employees are fired because of reduced volume, not because automation has been introduced. But when the fluctuation is on the recovery side, no new hirings are made; thus the statistics classify the original firings as a result of declining business conditions rather than reduced need for personnel because of equipment and system changes. This method of releasing employees during declining business activity and not rehiring when business conditions improve is known as *silent firing*. In many service-type businesses, the turnover of young woman in clerical positions is quite high because they leave their jobs when their husbands are transferred or when they begin to raise a family. When automated data processing systems are introduced into such organizations, the young women who leave are not replaced; thus a high attrition rate eliminates any necessity for direct firings.

It should not be assumed that the introduction of automated systems always requires a reduction in the number of employees—often it is just the opposite. New data processing systems are not just substitutes to fulfill former business objectives (see p. 20); they usually enlarge the company's goals to include acquiring more and better information. When more data is involved, more input is usually needed; and as yet, most types of input preparation require human operators. Many large insurance companies found that conversion to large-scale computer operations increased rather than decreased the number of employees; the conversion was still profitable because more reliable data could be produced, and insurance companies base their existence on the reliability of data used for setting their insurance premium rates.

In general, there appears to be a tendency for office-type jobs to become more stable with reduced turnover of workers. In many instances, introduction of an automated data processing system requires that workers have more technical knowledge; and new highly specialized positions will be created. Persons with backgrounds in these relatively new job classifications are difficult to find and expensive to hire; hence, management must frequently train personnel for these new jobs at the company's own expense. To have worker turnover in these specialized positions for which management has spent considerable sums to train its personnel is a very costly affair. Also, most automated systems include expensive equipment which must operate at near maximum levels if it is to pay for itself. Therefore, it is to the advantage of management to reduce cyclical and seasonal employment fluctuations and to maintain a regular, constant work flow and staff.

Even though no dismissals may result from a changeover to automated data processing, changes in job functions and job titles may occur. Generally, two results are possible:

1. Work may be upgraded. (The computer will take over routine, repetitious, boring jobs and thus free workers for more creative and challenging tasks.)

2. Work may be downgraded. (The computer will be programmed to make decisions, but it will require large quantities of input data resulting from menial, manual clerical duties.)

The current trend in job classification is an upgrading of the work force. Of course, many routine jobs will remain routine with a mere change of equipment—clerk typists will be placed on keypunching machines, etc. But many positions will be upgraded as a result of the need for more technical knowledge and of the development of increased responsibilities because of the installation of extremely complex and expensive equipment.

With this trend to upgrade jobs has come an additional obstacle in the efforts of unions to organize clerical workers. In the past, unionization of office workers made little progress for, unlike factory workers, office workers tend to identify themselves with management. A further upgrading of jobs and responsibilities will increase the shift from the more susceptible blue-collar worker to the less susceptible white-collar worker. On the other hand, it is possible that increased uncertainty about job security because of automation will put a trump card in the hands of union organizers. Surely union officials will not overlook the advantages resulting from automation during their campaigns for a shorter work week with higher pay. Currently, office workers remain a very lucrative source of potential union members; and considerable expense and effort has been applied within the past few years to bring clerical workers into union ranks.

MORALE PROBLEMS

Uncertainty about the future usually is fertile ground for fear. In many instances, fear is the product of misunderstanding and lack of basic knowledge about a problem. And this is true about automation. To many persons, the term *automation* implies some degree of change; and people do not like to change if any uncertainty is involved or if change concerns something they know little about. In the past, clerical positions were somewhat stable compared to seasonal hirings and firings in factories; the clerical worker now realizes he faces the same threat as any other worker.

Many company executives are aware of the potential disturbing force of fear; and before any automation changeovers are made, employees are introduced to, and kept informed of, projected plans. Such information programs help eliminate emotion-packed rumors. Because the installation of an automated system means an upgrading of positions for many employees, a properly managed informational campaign may be presented so that the changeover will be accepted, and perhaps envied, by many employees. The interest which management shows in employee problems goes a long way in eliminating fear and gaining confidence. But two factors tend to instill doubt and anxiety regardless of the approach:

1. Employees generally have little or no background in automated data processing.

2. An abundance of evidence has been reported about job elimination and unemployment resulting from conversion to automated systems.

To clerical employees working with middle management, the conversion to automated data processing seems likely to improve their job status. And job status is a serious consideration. To many persons, a job title or job objective is more important than the amount of pay, as shown by the number of persons entering relatively low-paying jobs, such as teachers and public officials. But to people of limited ability or nearing retirement age, the psychological impact of being replaced by a machine is a severe shock to the sense of worth.

The problem to be considered is whether management will assume the responsibility of providing for its employees, or whether the status symbol of prompt installation of EDP systems will over-occupy its attention. True, installing automated data processing systems can improve the company image in the eyes of the customers —the "up-to-dateness" of handling customers' financial matters is an important consideration. Often, however, the status symbol is overemphasized, and glamor and prestige obscure the true needs. To remain competitive, companies must keep pace in data processing as well as in production; but some businesses now acknowledge that they were victims of "computeritis," joining the crowd of companies that computerized before their needs truly required the services of a computer.

TRAINING PROBLEMS

When a system is converted to automated data processing, job changes are bound to occur and new skills must be learned. When employees are dismissed because of job elimination, retraining is often needed before new employment is available. The unemployment problem does not involve the fired worker as much as the worker who is not hired because of canceled positions.

Since training personnel for automated data processing jobs takes longer because of the technology involved, trainees are carefully selected to minimize future labor turnover. Applicants are often placed into one of three categories:

1. Adaptable (young, willing—trained for new skills in advanced technology—usually promoted)

2. Moderately adaptable (trained for other existing jobs of a similar nature—holding action)

3. Unadaptable (lacks willingness, zest, ability, or youth—shifted to other organizations or demoted).

Not all persons who desire to enter retraining programs are capable. John I. Snyder, Jr., Chairman of the Board of Directors for U.S. Industries, Inc., recently attacked "the myth that those who lose their jobs to automation can be retrained and put into jobs requiring higher skills and paying more money. Not only are there fewer jobs available today, but many workers are not retrainable in the first place due to the level of intelligence, age or aptitude." *

Masses of workers cannot be easily assigned to jobs created by electronic data processing—circumstances are different from the time when there was a mass movement from farms to factories. Intellectual and educational requirements are high and demanding. The best candidates for retraining programs appear to be young, aggressive persons with creative qualities who have been with the organization long enough to know and understand the business in terms of its operations and objectives.

There is, however, another pool of workers for data processing training: young men and women graduating from high schools. Young people who will qualify themselves to handle business paperwork rapidly, accurately, and efficiently are the persons who can take advantage of this wide and exciting new concept in modern business. If high school graduates have any desire at all to enter the field of business in the future, they have no choice but to become acquainted with some of the basic techniques of modern data processing.

The day is past when the apprentice was content to spend several years in learning a trade because he knew that he was acquiring a skill which he could practice remuneratively and proudly all his normal working life.

. . . the new worker must face the high probability that he will have to be trained and retrained several times between graduation and retirement.

Somehow we must educate for change, must bring students to accept change as natural and to see security, not in an old skill previously learned and in seniority, but in adaptability to change, in the ability to learn new skills. . . . We need somehow to

* John I. Snyder, "Big Labor Hunts for the Hard Answers" (by Keith Wheeler), *Life*, 55:73 (July 19, 1963), 84.

shift the emphasis to the student's responsibility for learning, to acquiring the habit of self-education.*

And perhaps serious thought should be given to the extent one wishes to excel in the data processing field. Top positions are likely to go to those who have had extensive data processing training in colleges and universities.

> Today, with the increase in the number of courses and programs in computers for college students, it appears as if there will be few opportunities for people with only a high school education to advance far beyond routine programming work. In fact, many companies have set a policy that future programmers must have a college degree, typically in business administration, mathematics, engineering, or computer science.†

CONCLUSION

We are probably safe in concluding that, in the long run, automated data processing will help raise the standard of living, help provide more goods and services at lower costs, and contribute toward making a fuller life for most Americans. We can expect new service-type businesses to be created and current processing systems to undergo constant revision as new equipment and new technology are developed.

In the short run, complex problems confronting clerical workers can be directly or indirectly attributed to the automation revolution—unemployment, displacement, retraining, and worker morale are but a few of the problems deserving careful study.

To predict the future in such a dynamic society as ours is indeed risky, but a look into the crystal ball might reveal the following predictions as they pertain to automated data processing:

* "Education for Automation," A *Report by the Advisory Committee on Automation,* Pennsylvania Curriculum Improvement Series No. 2, Department of Public Instruction, Harrisburg, Pa., 1961, pp. 6–7.

† Richard N. Schmidt and William E. Meyers, *Introduction to Computer Science and Data Processing* (New York: Holt, Rinehart and Winston, Inc., 1965), p. 12.

1. The professional status of office workers will continue to be upgraded.

2. The demand for present and new job specialties will persist for some time. Persons qualifying as instrument technicians, system analysts, system engineers, and other technically oriented jobs will have little trouble finding steady employment at comfortable wages.

3. The wages paid office workers will increase and will tend to be based more on responsibilities assumed than on output produced.

4. The employment will become steadier and more regular; and the regularity of night work will increase.

5. The length of training and retraining required for employment will increase.

6. The seniority concept will be deemphasized in lieu of merit recognition based on past performances and willingness to learn.

7. The unskilled, older worker will have increasing difficulty in entering and remaining in office occupations.

REVIEW QUESTIONS

True–False

1. Unemployment among clerical workers is a direct result attributed only to increased automation in the office.

2. Clerical workers are likely to be completely unionized in the near future if automated data processing continues to be adopted in modern business offices.

3. The true answer to unemployment in clerical positions is a sound retraining program for all persons affected as a result of automated data processing systems being installed in offices.

4. Once a clerical worker accepts retraining and becomes proficient

in the operation of automated data processing equipment, there will be little need for any additional retraining in the future.

5. As electronic data processing equipment is introduced into business offices, operators of the equipment tend to identify themselves more and more with middle management.

Multiple Choice

1. One major problem hindering solutions to clerical unemployment problems is

   a. Automation in the office is only ten years old.
   b. Management prefers to follow past traditions and practices and has no interest in its workers.
   c. Clerical workers are not as thoroughly unionized as other trades.
   d. Adequate research is not generally available for formulating policies to cope with unemployment resulting from automation in the office.

2. Automated data processing in the office as compared to automated production in the factory

   a. In terms of development and application is much ahead of factory production.
   b. Is easier to install once a new system has been designed.
   c. Would downgrade tasks to a similar or greater extent than the downgrading on production lines following automation.
   d. Has its own peculiarities, and solutions to personnel problems in the factory are not necessarily applicable to personnel problems in the office.

3. The failure of companies to refill job positions during economic prosperity that were previously vacated during a slack business period is called

   a. Silent firing
   b. Job replacement
   c. Inverse employment
   d. Job upgrading.

4. When businesses install large, new computer systems,

   a. Net profits will usually decrease.
   b. Efficiency of operations will normally reduce overall cost of processing data.
   c. Many clerical jobs will surely be lost.
   d. No absolute statement can be made referring to the effectiveness and efficiency of any one specific system.

5. There is a tendency for automated data processing to

a. Eliminate night work and overtime hours.
b. Place more emphasis on responsibility and ability and less emphasis on job security.
c. Maintain clerical wages at about the same level as before automated data processing was brought into the office.
d. Reduce the amount of training required for employment.

Discussion

1. What type of automated data processing employment exists in your community?

2. Do you believe the automation revolution in modern offices has had favorable or unfavorable effects on clerical workers? Explain.

3. What are some of the personnel problems you would attempt to resolve if you were a part of the management team and planned to introduce an EDP system in your office?

BIBLIOGRAPHY

Chapin, Ned, *An Introduction to Automatic Computers*. Princeton, N.J.: D. Van Nostrand Company, Inc., 1957.

Cordiner, Ralph (quoted by K. G. Matheson), "The Impact of the Computer on Curricula of Colleges of Business Administration," *Collegiate News and Views*, XIV, No. 4, May, 1961.

"Education for Automation," A *Report by the Advisory Committee on Automation*, Pennsylvania Curriculum Improvement Series No. 2, Department of Public Instruction, Harrisburg, Pa., 1961.

Nett, Roger, and Stanley A. Hetzler, *An Introduction to Electronic Data Processing*. Glencoe, Ill.: The Free Press, 1959.

Schmidt, Richard N., and William E. Meyers, *Introduction to Computer Science and Data Processing*. New York: Holt, Rinehart and Winston, Inc., 1965.

Snyder, John I., "Big Labor Hunts for the Hard Answers," *Life*, 55:73, July 19, 1963.

Webber, Wallace, "Office Automation Hits UAW," *Business Week*, Apr. 9, 1960.

Wiener, Norbert, "Is Automation Really a Job Killer?" *Business Week*, Feb. 24, 1962.

INDEX

Acceptability, (ADP function), 3, 15
Accounting board, 27-29
Accuracy
  input, 14
  tolerance, 15
Address, computer
  data, 149
  defined, 125
  instruction, 150
Address labels, 64
Addressograph plates (see Metal plates)
Aperture cards
  advantages, 87
  application, 40, 85-87
  filing, 87
Arithmetic unit
  defined, 172
  registers, 172
Automated data processing (ADP)
  defined, 7
  functions, 8, 13-18
Automatic typewriter
  application, 107
  code, 102
  mechanics, 103-7
Automation, defined, 7, 8

Banking, application, 14, 15, 195-98
Binary decimals
  number system, 94
  punched tape, 95, 96
Binary numbers, 95, 96
Bits
  core storage, 158
  defined, 158
  magnetic tape, 115
Block diagram, 141-45
Branching
  defined, 131
  procedure, 138-40, 185, 187

Carbon
  paper, 3, 26, 28
  spot, stripping, 27, 28

Card hopper, 60
Card sorter, 63
Cartridge, storage, 168
Cell, 157
Channel check, 101
Character reader
  credit card, 208
  defined, 203, 207
  direct input, 16
  MICR, 194-201
  numeric code, 207
Check digit, 197
Check row (see Parity)
  core storage, 157-58
  paper tape, 101
Code, Hollerith, 48, 50-52, 161
Code readers
  application, 205-6
  configuration, 204
  defined, 203
Coding
  deductions, 145
  IMCOM, 147-50
  operations, 147
  readers, 204, 207
Collection, data (ADP function), 13-14
Columns, punched card, 50
Common language
  IDP, 5, 8, 14, 47
  punched card, 48
  types, 47
Completeness, data (ADP function), 15
Computers
  arithmetic unit, 172-73, 178
  control unit, 170-72, 178
  data flow, 176-79
  input, 150, 177
  MICR, 198
  output, 174, 178
  storage, 156-61, 177-78
Computyper, 113
Constant data, 19, 20
Control unit, 170-72, 178

Core storage
  check row, 158
  defined, 156
  digit value, 156-59
Correctness, data (ADP function), 14
Costs, processing, 18, 21
Counter, 138
Credit cards, 204-9
Cue character, 194, 198, 200

Data
  address, 148
  cell, 169-70
  defined, 2
  itemization, 10
  manipulation, 10
  origination, 9
  quality, 21
  quantity, 21
  rearrangement, 3, 17
  reduction, quantity, 15
  refinement, 3
Data processing
  cycle, 8-12
  defined, 3
  functions, 13-17
  goals, 17-22
Diagramming
  block, 137, 141-45
  defined, 142
Displacement, 223-24

Edge-punched cards, 108-11
Electronic data processing (EDP)
  defined, 6, 8, 123
  history, 123
Elimination, processing steps, 18
Elimination, repetitive tasks, 19
Embossing
  ID plates, 204
  metal plates, 34, 35
Employment (ADP), 223
Error tolerance, 14, 15

Field, defined, 64, 65
Filmsort cards (see Aperture cards)
Flexowriter, 104-7
Form letters, 107, 108

Goals (ADP), 17-22
Graphotype, 36, 204

Hard copy, 174
Hollerith code, 48, 50-52, 161
Hopper, card, 60
Housekeeping, 154

IMCOM, defined, 146
Information
  defined, 2, 3, 11
  disposition, 12
  improvement, 21
  presentation, 11
Input
  ADP function, 9-10
  IMCOM, 150-56
  improvement, reading, 18
  speeds, 100
Instructions
  address, 149
  programming, 124
Integrated data processing (IDP)
  defined, 5-6, 8, 47
  introduction, 47
Interrelationship, 3, 8, 25
Interrelationship of systems and machines
  (IS&M)
  defined, 4, 8, 25
  introduction, 3, 25, 26
  goals, 26
Itemization, data, 10

Job training, 227-28
Job upgrading, 17, 225

Keypunching, equipment, 56-60
Keysorting, 29-34

Looping
  defined, 136
  major, minor, 142-43

Magnetic card, 167-69
Magnetic cores, 156-59
Magnetic disk, 165
Magnetic disk pack, 166-67
Magnetic drum, 163
Magnetic ink
  banking, 195-201
  defined, 194
  code, 194
  direct input, 15
  encoder, 197
  sorter-reader, 199-200
Magnetic tape
  code, 115
  physical characteristics, 114-16
  storage, 156
Mailing subscriptions, 18-19
Manipulation, data
  ADP function, 16
  processing cycle, 10-11
Mark-sense cards, 82-85
Mechanization, 5-6

Metal plates, 34-38
Micro-data cards (*see* Aperture cards)
Microfilming
    advantages, 43
    aperture, 41, 85-88
    film size, 40
    introduction, 38-39
    jackets, 41
    storage, 42-43
    viewers, 42

Name plates, 34-35
Number base, 92-93
Numeric keyboards, 59

Office automation, 7-8
On-line, 203
Operation code, 147-48
Optical readers (*see* Code, Character reader)
Organization, data, 9-10
Output
    ADP function, 17
    IMCOM, 174-76, 178
    speed, 17, 174

Parity, 158
Payroll processing
    pegboard, 27-29
    program, 130-41, 155, 183-93
    punched card, 61
Pegboard, 4, 27-29
Plane, storage, 159, 163
Port-a-Punch, 80-82
Presentation, information, 11
Printers, 17, 76, 78, 174
Processing, (ADP function), 3, 16
Program, stored, 129, 150
Program card, 69-73
Program drum, 72-73
Programming
    addressing, 125, 148-49
    branching, 131
    coding, 146-50
    concept, 124-25
    diagramming, 137, 139, 141-45
    looping, 136-37
Punch dies, 57
Punched cards
    advantages, disadvantages, 79-80
    design, 73-76
    history, 48
    Hollerith code, 50-52
    operation principle, 48-49
    physical characteristics, 52-56
    punching equipment, 56-61
Punched edge card, 108-11

Punch marker, 89
Punched tags, tickets
    codes, 89, 91
    direct input, 15
    introduction, 88-90
    merchandising, 90-92
Punched tape
    advantages, 99
    binary numbers, 95
    channel check, 101
    channels, 95
    codes, 100-102
    history, 97
    introduction, 97
    mechanics, 49

Rearrangement, (ADP function), 16
Register, 172-73
Reproducer, card, 74, 83
Rows, punched card, 51

School accounting, 30-33, 68, 86
Shifting, 139
Sign bit, 157-58
Silent firing, 224
Sorter
    punched card, 63
    MICR, 198-99
Source document
    input, 13-14, 16, 30
    sequence in cycle, 9-10
Spot carbon, 27
Storage
    core, 156
    defined, 156, 163
    magnetic disk, 165
    magnetic disk pack, 166-67
    magnetic drum, 163
    planes, 159
Stored program, 129, 150
System, defined, 3, 25

Telegrams, 97, 107-8
Typewriters
    automatic, 104, 112
    electric, 8

Uni-Kard, jacket, 41

Variable data, 20
Verification, (ADP function), 14

Word
    defined, 65
    IMCOM, 146-50
Writing board, 27-29

Zones, punched card, 51